Holiday Celebrations

with recipes from Younkers

Home for the Holidays

Memories make the holidays special: the warmth of a roaring fire, the laughter of friends, a child's gleeful anticipation, the return to a familiar hometown. And, of all holiday traditions, none is more special than the holiday meal. There, at your family table, the celebration takes shape with time-honored recipes, special dishes shared only once a year with those who mean the most to you.

As your hometown store, we hope that we have contributed to your holiday memories over the years. To continue that tradition, we've collected our favorite tried-and-true holiday recipes as well as some new culinary ideas for your special family celebrations. Many come directly from the chefs of the Younkers Tea Room, a cornerstone of our downtown Des Moines store for 88 years. We hope that over time these favorites of the Younkers family will become favorites of yours as well.

We wish you and your family a joyous holiday season filled with treasured moments, delightful surprises, and lasting memories.

Happy Holidays!

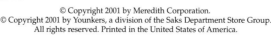

Published by Meredith® Books, Publishing Group of Meredith Corporation.
1716 Locust Street, Des Moines, IA 50309-3023

First Edition
ISBN: 0-696-21488-1

Table of Contents

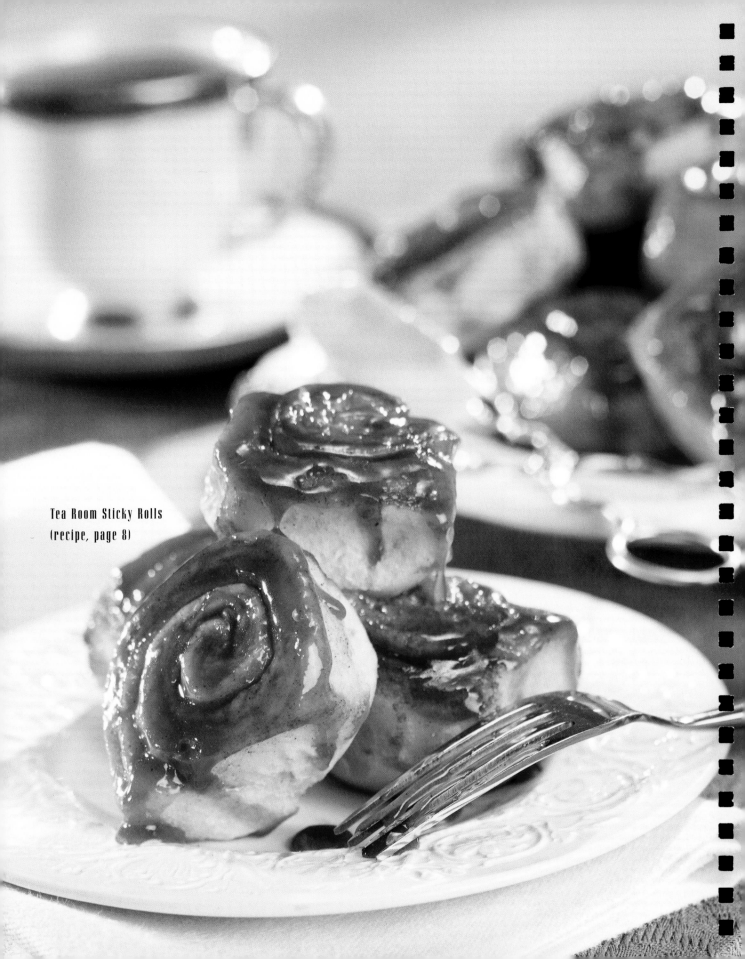

Tea Room Sticky Rolls
(recipe, page 8)

Younkers Classics

The holidays are a cherished time of year. Turn to this special recipe section from Younkers to help complete your celebration. Whether it's an appetizer party, weekend brunch, or festive dinner, great food is the centerpiece of the occasion. The recipes here include favorites of generations of Midwestern families, as well as some dishes with fun, new twists on the classics.

Tea Room
Chicken Salad

Tea Room Chicken Salad

3 cups diced, cooked
   chicken thighs
1 cup chopped celery
¼ cup chopped onion
¼ cup shelled sunflower
   seeds
1 cup ranch salad
   dressing
1 teaspoon celery salt
½ teaspoon dried minced
   garlic
   Salt and black pepper
   (optional)

1 In a large bowl combine chicken, celery, onion, and sunflower seeds. For dressing, in a small bowl stir together salad dressing, celery salt, and garlic. If desired, season to taste with salt and black pepper. Pour dressing over chicken mixture; toss to mix well. Cover and chill for 1 hour. Makes 6 servings.

Nutrition Facts per serving: 379 cal., 31 g total fat (6 g sat. fat), 68 mg chol., 816 mg sodium, 5 g carbo., 1 g fiber, 20 g pro.
Daily Values: 2% vit. A, 4% vit. C, 3% calcium, 8% iron

Braised Lamb Shanks

1 cup all-purpose flour
8 meaty lamb shanks
   (¾ to 1 pound each)
½ cup olive oil or cooking
   oil
4 carrots, diced
4 stalks celery, cut into
   ½-inch pieces
2 medium tomatoes,
   halved crosswise and
   quartered
1 medium onion, cut up
12 cloves garlic
3 bay leaves
1 6-inch sprig fresh
   rosemary
1 teaspoon cracked black
   pepper
4 cups lamb or beef broth
   Hot cooked orzo,
   noodles, or mashed
   potatoes
   Gremolada

1 Combine the flour, 1 teaspoon *salt*, and ½ teaspoon *black pepper* in a shallow dish. Coat the shanks with the flour mixture. In a roasting pan large enough to hold all the shanks in a single layer, brown the shanks on all sides in hot oil. Remove the shanks. Add carrots, celery, tomatoes, onion, and garlic to pan. Cook, stirring occasionally, until the onions are tender.

2 Place the shanks on top of the vegetable mixture. Add bay leaves, rosemary, cracked black pepper, and 1 teaspoon *salt*. Pour broth over meat. Bake, covered, in a 350° oven for 2 to 3 hours or until the meat falls off the bone easily and the sauce in the pan is like gravy. Remove bay leaves and rosemary. Serve shanks with the gravy and orzo, noodles, or mashed potatoes. Garnish with Gremolada. Makes 8 servings.

Gremolada: In a small bowl combine 1 clove *garlic,* minced; 2 teaspoons finely shredded *lemon peel;* 1 tablespoon snipped fresh Italian *parsley;* and 10 *anchovy* fillets, finely chopped. Cover and chill up to 3 hours.

Nutrition Facts per serving: 580 cal., 24 g total fat (5 g sat. fat), 153 mg chol., 1,326 mg sodium, 34 g carbo., 4 g fiber, 55 g pro.
Daily Values: 312% vit. A, 23% vit. C, 7% calcium, 38% iron

Tea Room Sticky Rolls

4 to 4 1/3 cups all-purpose
flour
1 package active dry
yeast
1 cup milk
1/3 cup sugar
1/3 cup butter or
margarine
1/2 teaspoon salt
2 eggs
Caramel Smear
Cinnamon Spread

1 In a large mixing bowl combine 2 cups of the the flour and the yeast; set aside.

2 In a medium saucepan heat and stir milk, sugar, butter or margarine, and salt just until warm (120° to 130°) and butter or margarine almost melts. Add milk mixture to dry mixture along with eggs. Beat with an electric mixer on low to medium speed for 30 seconds, scraping bowl. Beat on high speed for 3 minutes. Using a wooden spoon, stir in as much of the remaining flour as you can.

3 Turn dough out onto a lightly floured surface. Knead in enough remaining flour to make a moderately soft dough that is smooth and elastic (3 to 5 minutes total). Shape dough into a ball. Place dough in a lightly greased bowl; turn once to grease dough. Cover and let rise in a warm place until double in size (about 1 hour).

4 Punch dough down. Turn out onto a lightly floured surface. Divide in half. Cover and let rest 10 minutes. Spread a 15×10×1-inch baking pan evenly with Caramel Smear.

5 Roll each portion of dough into an 24×6-inch rectangle about 1/8 inch thick. Spread half of the Cinnamon Spread over each rectangle to within 1 inch of the edges. Roll up, starting from a long side. Seal seam. Cut into 1-inch slices. Place about 1 inch apart in prepared pan. Cover and let rise in a warm place until nearly double (about 30 minutes).

6 Bake in a 350° oven for 20 to 30 minutes or until golden. Remove from oven and let cool 5 minutes. Turn the pan of rolls over onto another 15×10-inch pan so the caramel is on top. Serve warm. Makes 40 rolls.

Caramel Smear: In a mixing bowl combine 1/3 cup *butter,* melted; 1 cup packed *brown sugar;* 1/4 cup light-colored *corn syrup;* 3/4 teaspoon *ground cinnamon;* and 1/4 teaspoon *salt.* Stir until smooth.

Cinnamon Spread: In a small mixing bowl stir together 3/4 cup packed *brown sugar,* 1 tablespoon *cooking oil,* 1 tablespoon light-colored *corn syrup,* and 1/2 teaspoon *ground cinnamon.*

Nutrition Facts per roll: 130 cal., 4 g total fat (2 g sat. fat), 20 mg chol., 90 mg sodium, 22 g carbo., 0 g fiber, 2 g pro.
Daily Values: 3% vit. A, 2% calcium, 4% iron

Tea Room Rarebit Sauce

⅓ cup cooking oil
⅓ cup all-purpose flour
1 teaspoon paprika
¼ teaspoon salt
¼ teaspoon dry mustard
2 cups whole or reduced-fat milk
1 teaspoon Worcestershire sauce
¼ teaspoon bottled hot pepper sauce
1 cup shredded process sharp American cheese (4 ounces)

1 Place oil in a medium saucepan. Stir together flour, paprika, salt, and dry mustard. Add flour mixture to oil; cook and stir for 1 minute. Stir in milk all at once. Cook and stir over medium heat until thickened and bubbly. Cook and stir 1 minute more. Remove from heat; stir in Worcestershire sauce and hot pepper sauce. Add cheese and stir until melted. Makes 2 cups.

Nutrition Facts per ¼-cup serving: 190 cal., 16 g total fat (5 g sat. fat), 22 mg chol., 313 mg sodium, 7 g carbo., 0 g fiber, 6 g pro.
Daily Values: 8% vit. A, 2% vit. C, 17% calcium, 3% iron

Note: To make Younkers' popular Rarebit Burgers, cook 8 hamburger patties to 170° or until no pink remains. Place each burger in a toasted hamburger bun. Spoon about ¼ cup of Rarebit Sauce over each bun. Serve immediately.

Grilled Lamb Sirloin

4 6- to 8-ounce lamb sirloin or top round steaks
½ cup olive oil
¼ cup red wine vinegar
1 teaspoon snipped fresh basil
½ teaspoon cracked black pepper
½ teaspoon finely shredded lemon peel
¼ teaspoon kosher salt
2 cloves garlic, minced
Parmesan Mashed Potatoes

1 Trim fat from steaks. Place steaks in a large self-sealing plastic bag. In a bowl combine olive oil, vinegar, basil, pepper, lemon peel, salt, and garlic. Pour over meat in bag; seal bag. Marinate in the refrigerator for 8 hours or overnight.

2 Drain steaks, discarding marinade. Grill or broil steaks to desired doneness. Serve with Parmesan Mashed Potatoes. Makes 4 servings.

Parmesan Mashed Potatoes: In a large pan of boiling water cook 4 to 6 quartered, peeled medium *potatoes* until tender. Drain. Mash with a potato masher or beat with an electric mixer on low speed. Add one 8-ounce carton *dairy sour cream*, ¼ cup grated *Parmesan cheese*, ¼ cup *milk*, and *salt* and *black pepper* to taste. Mash or beat mixture until smooth and fluffy.

Nutrition Facts per serving: 433 cal., 25 g total fat (11 g sat. fat), 75 mg chol., 400 mg sodium, 31 g carbo., 3 g fiber, 21 g pro.
Daily Values: 11% vit. A, 19% vit. C, 19% calcium, 9% iron

Wilted Spinach Salad

Wilted Spinach Salad

8 cups washed, stemmed spinach
1 cup sliced fresh mushrooms
4 slices bacon, diced
1 medium onion, chopped (½ cup)
½ cup Dijon-style mustard
½ cup packed brown sugar
½ cup dry white wine
½ cup rice or other mild, light-colored vinegar
4 hard-cooked eggs, chopped

1 In a large salad bowl toss together spinach and mushrooms; set aside.

2 In a large skillet, cook the bacon over medium heat for 3 minutes. Add onion and cook until the bacon is crisp and onion is tender. Drain, reserving 3 tablespoons drippings in the skillet. Add the mustard, brown sugar, wine, and vinegar; bring to boiling. Reduce heat and simmer about 5 minutes or until slightly thickened. Remove from heat; cool slightly.

3 Pour dressing over spinach and mushrooms; toss until combined and spinach is slightly wilted. Add hard-cooked eggs; toss gently. Serve at once. Makes 6 servings.

Nutrition Facts per serving: 268 cal., 14 g total fat (4 g sat. fat), 151 mg chol., 264 mg sodium, 24 g carbo., 2 g fiber, 9 g pro.
Daily Values: 55% vit. A, 18% vit. C, 10% calcium, 15% iron

Asparagus and Orange Salad

1½ pounds fresh asparagus spears
1 cup olive oil
¼ cup Dijon-style mustard
¼ cup orange juice
2 teaspoons rice vinegar
1 teaspoon snipped fresh parsley
Salt and black pepper
4 oranges, peeled and sectioned
1 small red onion, thinly sliced and separated into rings

1 Snap off and discard woody bases from asparagus. Cut the spears into 2-inch pieces. Cook in boiling water in a large saucepan for 1 minute; drain. Cool immediately in a bowl of ice water. Drain on paper towels.

2 For dressing, in a large bowl slowly add olive oil to mustard in a thin stream, whisking constantly until all the oil is incorporated and the consistency is like mayonnaise. Whisk in orange juice, vinegar, and parsley. Season with salt and black pepper to taste.

3 In a large bowl toss together asparagus and dressing; add orange sections and onion rings; toss gently. Cover and chill 1 hour before serving. Makes 6 servings.

Nutrition Facts per serving: 398 cal., 37 g total fat (5 g sat. fat), 0 mg chol., 164 mg sodium, 14 g carbo., 3 g fiber, 4 g pro.
Daily Values: 6% vit. A, 111% vit. C, 6% calcium, 5% iron

Yule Log
(Bûche de Noël)

Yule Log (Bûche de Noël)

1 cup all-purpose flour
1 tablespoon
   unsweetened cocoa
   powder
1 teaspoon baking
   powder
3 eggs
¾ cup sugar
½ cup milk
2 tablespoons butter
1 teaspoon honey
   Chocolate Filling
   Rich Chocolate Frosting
   Green and red frosting
   (optional)

1 Grease and lightly flour (or line with waxed paper and lightly grease) a 15×10×1-inch baking pan; set aside. Stir together flour, cocoa powder, and baking powder; set aside.

2 In a mixing bowl beat eggs with an electric mixer on high speed about 4 minutes or until thick. Gradually add sugar, beating on medium speed for 4 to 5 minutes or until light and fluffy. Add the dry mixture; beat on low to medium speed just until combined.

3 In a small saucepan heat and stir milk, butter, and honey until butter melts; add to batter, beating until combined. Pour batter into the prepared pan; spread evenly.

4 Bake in a 350° oven for 15 to 20 minutes or until top springs back. Immediately loosen cake from pan. Invert cake onto a towel sprinkled with cocoa powder. (Remove waxed paper, if used.) Roll up warm cake and towel, starting from a short side. Cool on a wire rack. Gently unroll cake. Spread Chocolate Filling on cake to within 1 inch of edges. Reroll cake. Cover and refrigerate for 30 minutes.

5 Cut a small diagonal slice from each end of the log. Frost cake with Rich Chocolate Frosting. Place trimmed pieces on the log to look like trimmed branches or knots; frost. Using tines of a fork, score frosting lengthwise to resemble tree bark. If desired, decorate with green frosting leaves and red frosting berries. Store in refrigerator. Makes 10 servings.

Chocolate Filling: In a small mixing bowl stir together ¼ cup *powdered sugar* and ¼ cup *unsweetened cocoa powder*. Stir in 1 cup *whipping cream* and ½ teaspoon *vanilla* until smooth. Chill at least 15 minutes. Beat with chilled beaters of an electric mixer on medium speed until soft peaks form (tips curl).

Rich Chocolate Frosting: In a medium saucepan heat and stir 3 ounces *unsweetened chocolate* and 3 tablespoons *butter* until chocolate melts. Remove from heat. Stir in 1½ cups sifted *powdered sugar*, ¼ cup *milk*, and 1 teaspoon *vanilla*. Add 1½ cups additional *powdered sugar* and enough *milk* to make of spreading consistency (1 to 2 tablespoons).

Nutrition Facts per serving: 454 cal., 22 g total fat (13 g sat. fat), 115 mg chol., 142 mg sodium, 62 g carbo., 2 g fiber, 6 g pro.
Daily Values: 15% vit. A, 1% vit. C, 11% calcium, 9% iron

Coconut Fried Shrimp
(recipe, page 16)

Phyllo Cups with Black Beans
(recipe, page 17)

Jerk Chicken Skewers
(recipe, page 16)

Open House

Share the magic of the holidays by entertaining friends with an open house ... a casual appetizer party with a buffet of serve-yourself snacks and beverages. Many of these tempting recipes can be made ahead or are simple enough to put together just before the guests arrive. Stir in some festive music and fun decorations, and you will be ready for a memorable time.

Coconut Fried Shrimp

1 8-ounce carton dairy
   sour cream
2 tablespoons chutney
   (snip any large pieces)
1 tablespoon honey
2 teaspoons curry powder
   Cooking oil for deep-
   fat frying
1½ pounds fresh shrimp in
   shells (32 to 36 large)
1 egg yolk
1 cup ice-cold water
1 cup all-purpose flour
1 cup shredded coconut
2 tablespoons cornstarch
2 egg whites
½ cup cornstarch
   Mesclun or salad greens

1 For sauce, combine sour cream, chutney, honey, and curry powder. Cover and refrigerate 1 hour or overnight to allow flavors to blend.

2 Heat 3 to 4 inches oil in a large saucepan or deep fryer to 365°. Peel and devein shrimp, leaving tails intact.

3 For batter, stir together egg yolk and water; set aside. In a large bowl combine flour, coconut, and the 2 tablespoons cornstarch; set aside. In a small bowl beat egg whites until stiff peaks form (tips stand straight). Stir the egg yolk mixture into dry ingredients just until moistened. Fold in beaten egg whites. (Do not allow batter to stand more than 10 to 15 minutes before using.)

4 Coat shrimp with the ½ cup cornstarch. Holding shrimp by the tails with tongs, dip in batter, leaving tails uncoated. Allow excess batter to drain back into bowl. Fry shrimp, 3 or 4 at a time, for 2½ to 3 minutes or until shrimp are done and batter is lightly golden, turning once. Drain on paper towels. Serve shrimp on mesclun-lined platter. Pass sauce for dipping. Makes 8 servings.

Nutrition Facts per serving: 319 cal., 15 g total fat (8 g sat. fat), 136 mg chol., 133 mg sodium, 29 g carbo., 2 g fiber, 17 g pro.
Daily Values: 11% vit. A, 6% vit. C, 8% calcium, 14% iron

Jerk Chicken Skewers

⅓ cup bottled teriyaki
   sauce
3 tablespoons water
½ teaspoon Jamaican jerk
   seasoning
1 pound skinless,
   boneless chicken
   breasts, cut into
   3×1-inch pieces
20 5- to 6-inch wooden
   skewers
1 large sweet potato
   (12 to 16 ounces)
1 medium green sweet
   pepper, cut into 1-inch
   pieces

1 For marinade, in a small bowl combine teriyaki sauce, water, and jerk seasoning. Place chicken in a self-sealing plastic bag set into a shallow dish. Pour marinade over chicken. Seal bag; turn to coat chicken. Marinate in the refrigerator for 2 to 4 hours, turning bag occasionally. Soak wooden skewers in water for 30 minutes.

2 Meanwhile, peel sweet potato and cut into 1-inch cubes. Cook potato in lightly salted water, covered, for 6 minutes or until just tender, adding sweet pepper pieces the last 2 minutes. Drain potato and pepper. Set aside.

3 Drain chicken, reserving marinade. Thread 1 piece each of the chicken, potato, and pepper onto each skewer, threading chicken strips accordion-style. Brush kabobs with marinade.

4 Place kabobs on the unheated rack of a broiler pan. Broil 5 to 6 inches from the heat about 10 minutes or until the chicken is tender and no longer pink, turning once. Or, grill kabobs on the rack of an uncovered grill directly over medium-hot coals for 8 to 10 minutes or until chicken is tender and no longer pink, turning once halfway through grilling. Makes 20 skewers.

Nutrition Facts per skewer: 47 cal., 0 g total fat, 13 mg chol., 122 mg sodium, 5 g carbo., 1 g fiber, 6 g pro.
Daily Values: 62% vit. A, 11% vit. C, 1% calcium, 2% iron

Lemon-Marinated Vegetables

Lemon Vinaigrette
8 ounces fresh green beans, trimmed
12 ounces baby carrots with tops, peeled and trimmed
2 medium red and/or yellow sweet peppers, cut into 1-inch pieces
8 ounces fresh mushrooms, stems removed
1 cup cherry tomatoes

1 Prepare Lemon Vinaigrette; set aside. In a large saucepan cook green beans, covered, in a small amount of boiling water for 4 minutes. Add carrots and cook, covered, for 8 minutes more or until vegetables are crisp-tender. Drain and rinse with cold water. Combine beans, carrots, sweet peppers, mushrooms, and tomatoes in a large self-sealing plastic bag set in a large bowl. Pour Lemon Vinaigrette over vegetables.

2 Seal bag and refrigerate for 4 to 24 hours, turning bag occasionally. To serve, bring to room temperature. Drain vegetables; arrange on a platter. Makes 8 to 10 servings.

Lemon Vinaigrette: In a screw-top jar combine $1/3$ cup *olive oil* or *cooking oil*; $1/3$ cup fresh *lemon juice*; 2 tablespoons snipped *fresh basil*; 1 clove *garlic*, minced; 1 tablespoon *Dijon-style mustard*; $1/8$ teaspoon *salt*; and $1/8$ teaspoon *black pepper*. Cover and shake well.

Nutrition Facts per serving: 97 cal., 6 g total fat (1 g sat. fat), 0 mg chol., 67 mg sodium, 11 g carbo., 3 g fiber, 3 g pro.
Daily Values: 251% vit. A, 93% vit. C, 3% calcium, 5% iron

Phyllo Cups with Black Beans

4 sheets (18×14 inches) frozen phyllo dough, thawed
$1/4$ cup butter or margarine, melted
Nonstick cooking spray
$1/4$ cup finely chopped onion
$1/4$ cup finely chopped celery
$1/2$ cup diced smoked ham or crumbled cooked bacon
$1/4$ cup shredded carrot
$1/2$ teaspoon instant chicken bouillon granules
1 cup canned black beans, drained and rinsed
$1/4$ cup water
2 teaspoons lime juice

1 Lightly brush one sheet of phyllo dough with some of the melted butter or margarine. Place another sheet of phyllo on top of the first sheet and brush with butter or margarine. Keep remaining phyllo covered with plastic wrap to keep from drying out. Repeat with remaining phyllo and butter or margarine. Cut phyllo stack lengthwise into three 18-inch-long strips. Cut each strip crosswise into 6 rectangles.

2 Press each rectangle into a greased $1\frac{3}{4}$-inch muffin cup, pleating as needed to fit. Bake in a 350° oven for 8 to 10 minutes or until golden. Cool for 5 minutes in pan. Remove from pan; cool completely on wire rack. (Phyllo cups may be made ahead and stored, tightly covered, at room temperature overnight or frozen up to 1 month.)

3 Meanwhile, spray a cold, large skillet with nonstick coating. Heat over medium heat until hot. Add onion and celery; cook 3 to 5 minutes or until tender. Stir in ham or bacon, carrot, bouillon granules, beans, water, and lime juice. Cook, uncovered, about 3 minutes more or until heated through. Spoon hot filling into phyllo cups. Serve immediately. Makes 18 cups.

Nutrition Facts per cup: 56 cal., 3 g total fat (2 g sat. fat), 10 mg chol., 171 mg sodium, 5 g carbo., 1 g fiber, 2 g pro.
Daily Values: 11% vit. A, 1% vit. C, 1% calcium, 2% iron

Cheese, Walnut, and Pear Crostini

Cheese, Walnut, and Pear Crostini

4 ounces crumbled
  blue cheese
2 tablespoons unsalted
  butter
2 tablespoons brandy
¼ cup chopped walnuts
16 ¼-inch-thick toasted
  French bread slices or
  baguette slices
1 medium ripe pear,
  cored and thinly sliced

1 In a small bowl let the blue cheese and butter stand at room temperature about 30 minutes. Mash with a fork until well combined. Stir in brandy and chopped walnuts. Top each slice of bread with a pear slice. Top each pear slice with 1 tablespoon of the blue cheese mixture.

2 Place bread slices on a baking sheet. Broil 4 to 5 inches from heat about 2 minutes or until the cheese is melted and bubbly. Serve hot. Makes 8 to 12 servings.

Nutrition Facts per serving: 201 cal., 10 g total fat (5 g sat. fat), 19 mg chol., 371 mg sodium, 19 g carbo., 2 g fiber, 6 g pro.

Daily Values: 4% vit. A, 1% vit. C, 10% calcium, 5% iron

White Bean Dip

¼ cup soft bread crumbs
2 tablespoons dry white
  wine or water
1 15- to 19-ounce can
  cannellini beans or
  Great Northern beans,
  drained and rinsed
¼ cup slivered almonds,
  toasted
2 tablespoons lemon
  juice
2 tablespoons olive oil
¼ teaspoon salt
⅛ teaspoon ground red
  pepper
3 cloves garlic, minced
2 teaspoons snipped
  fresh oregano or basil
  or ½ teaspoon dried
  oregano or basil,
  crushed
  Tortilla chips and
  assorted vegetable
  dippers

1 Combine bread crumbs and wine or water; set aside to soak for 10 minutes.

2 In a food processor bowl or blender container combine beans, almonds, lemon juice, olive oil, salt, red pepper, and garlic. Cover and process or blend until almost smooth. Add bread crumb mixture; blend until smooth. Stir in the oregano or basil. Cover and chill for 4 to 24 hours.

3 To serve, transfer to a serving bowl. Serve with tortilla chips and vegetable dippers. Makes 2 cups dip.

Nutrition Facts per tablespoon dip: 22 cal., 1 g total fat (0 g sat. fat), 0 mg chol., 23 mg sodium, 2 g carbo., 1 g fiber, 1 g pro.

Daily Values: 1% vit. C, 1% iron

Appetizer Cheesecake

1/4 cup butter or
    margarine, melted
6 sheets (18×14 inches)
    frozen phyllo dough,
    thawed
1/2 of a 6-ounce jar
    marinated artichoke
    hearts
3 8-ounce packages
    cream cheese, softened
1 1/4 cups crumbled feta
    cheese (5 ounces)
1/2 teaspoon dried
    oregano, crushed
1/4 teaspoon garlic powder
3 eggs
1/4 cup sliced green onions

1 For crust, brush bottom and sides of a 9-inch springform pan with some of the melted butter or margarine. Unroll phyllo dough; cover with plastic wrap. Remove 1 sheet of phyllo and cut into a 13-inch circle. Ease the circle into the prepared pan off-center so that phyllo extends 3 inches up side of pan. Brush with melted butter or margarine. Repeat with remaining phyllo and remaining butter or margarine, placing sheets off-center to cover bottom and side of pan. Make 2 slits in the center of phyllo for steam to escape.

2 Bake in a 400° oven 9 to 10 minutes or until light golden brown. Cool on a wire rack. Lower oven temperature to 325°.

3 Meanwhile, drain and chop artichokes, reserving 2 tablespoons of the marinade; set aside.

4 In a large mixing bowl beat cream cheese with an electric mixer until smooth. Add feta, oregano, and garlic powder. Beat well. Add eggs; beat just until combined. Do not overbeat. Stir in artichoke hearts, reserved marinade, and green onions. Pour into the crust. Bake in a 325° oven for 35 to 40 minutes or until center is soft-set and outside stays firm when gently shaken. Cool.

5 Cover; refrigerate for at least 2 hours or for up to 24 hours. To serve, remove from pan and, if desired, let stand to bring to room temperature or serve immediately. Cut into wedges. Makes 14 servings.

Nutrition Facts per serving: 273 cal., 24 g total fat (13 g sat. fat), 108 mg chol., 368 mg sodium, 7 g carbo., 0 g fiber, 7 g pro.
Daily Values: 29% vit. A, 2% vit. C, 8% calcium, 7% iron

Beef Satay with Peanut Sauce

1 pound lean boneless beef sirloin steak, cut 1 inch thick and trimmed of separable fat
1 small onion, cut up
2 tablespoons reduced-sodium soy sauce
2 tablespoons lime juice
1 teaspoon sugar
1 teaspoon ground cumin
1 clove garlic, minced
1/4 cup reduced-sodium chicken broth
2 tablespoons peanut butter
1 tablespoon molasses or honey
1 teaspoon soy sauce
1/8 to 1/4 teaspoon crushed red pepper
1 clove garlic, minced

1 Cut beef into 1¼-inch pieces. Place in a self-sealing plastic bag set in a deep bowl.

2 For marinade, in a food processor bowl or blender container place onion, the 2 tablespoons soy sauce, lime juice, sugar, cumin, and garlic. Cover; process or blend until smooth. Pour over meat in bag; close bag. Marinate meat in the refrigerator about 4 hours, turning bag occasionally.

3 For Peanut Sauce, in a saucepan gradually stir chicken broth into peanut butter. Stir in molasses or honey, the 1 teaspoon soy sauce, crushed red pepper, and garlic. Cook and stir until heated through. Keep warm.

4 Drain meat, discarding marinade. Thread meat onto 4 skewers, leaving ¼-inch space between pieces. Arrange skewers on the unheated rack of a broiler pan. Broil 3 to 4 inches from the heat for 7 to 9 minutes or until desired doneness, turning occasionally to brown evenly. Serve meat with Peanut Sauce for dipping. Makes 8 servings.

Nutrition Facts per serving: 109 cal., 4 g total fat (1 g sat. fat), 34 mg chol., 163 mg sodium, 4 g carbo., 0 g fiber, 13 g pro.
Daily Values: 2% vit. C, 2% calcium, 10% iron

Smoky Cheese Ball

2 8-ounce packages cream cheese
2 cups shredded smoked cheddar, Swiss, or Gouda cheese
1/2 cup butter or margarine, softened
2 tablespoons milk
2 teaspoons steak sauce
1 cup finely chopped nuts, toasted

1 Bring cheeses and butter or margarine to room temperature. Add milk and steak sauce; beat until fluffy. Cover; chill for 4 to 24 hours. Shape mixture into a ball. Roll in nuts. Let stand for 15 minutes. Serve with assorted crackers. Makes 3½ cups.

Nutrition Facts per tablespoon spread: 74 cal., 7 g total fat (3 g sat. fat), 13 mg chol., 72 mg sodium, 1 g carbo., 0 g fiber, 2 g pro.
Daily Values: 6% vit. A, 3% calcium, 1% iron

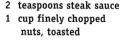

Corn-Cheese Dip

Corn-Cheese Dip

½ cup dairy sour cream
½ cup mayonnaise or salad dressing
⅓ cup picante sauce
¼ teaspoon black pepper
⅛ teaspoon garlic powder
3 cups cheddar cheese, shredded (12 ounces)
1 12-ounce can whole kernel corn, rinsed and drained
¼ cup seeded and chopped jalapeño pepper
Dairy sour cream (optional)
Tiny chile pepper (optional)
Corn tortilla chips, corn chips, or crackers

1 In a large bowl stir together sour cream, mayonnaise or salad dressing, picante sauce, black pepper, and garlic powder. Stir in cheese, corn, and jalapeño pepper. Cover and chill at least 2 hours.

2 To serve, dollop with sour cream and top with a chile pepper, if desired. Serve with tortilla chips, corn chips, or crackers. Makes 4 cups dip.

Nutrition Facts per 2-tablespoon serving: 154 cal., 10 g total fat (4 g sat. fat), 14 mg chol., 180 mg sodium, 12 g carbo., 1 g fiber, 4 g pro.

Daily Values: 3% vit. A, 4% vit. C, 8% calcium, 3% iron

Note: Because jalapeño peppers contain volatile oils that can burn your skin and eyes, wear plastic or rubber gloves when working with them. If your bare hands touch the peppers, wash your hands well with soap and water.

Crab Cakes

1 6- to 8-ounce package frozen lump crabmeat or one 6-ounce can crabmeat, drained, flaked, and cartilage removed
1 egg, slightly beaten
6 tablespoons fine dry bread crumbs
2 tablespoons finely chopped carrot
2 tablespoons finely chopped celery
1 tablespoon finely chopped green onion (green part only; chop and set aside the white part for the Tartar Sauce)
2 tablespoons mayonnaise or salad dressing
¾ teaspoon dry mustard
¼ teaspoon bottled hot pepper sauce
2 tablespoons cooking oil
Tartar Sauce

1 Thaw crabmeat in the refrigerator, if frozen; drain. In a medium mixing bowl combine egg, 4 tablespoons of the bread crumbs, the carrot, celery, onion, mayonnaise or salad dressing, dry mustard, and hot pepper sauce. Gently stir in crabmeat just until combined. With wet hands, gently shape mixture into eight ½-inch-thick patties, about 2 inches in diameter.

2 Place remaining crumbs in a shallow dish. Coat both sides of the patties with crumbs.

3 In a large skillet heat oil over medium heat. Add crab cakes. Cook about 3 minutes on each side or until golden brown and heated through. Serve immediately with Tartar Sauce. Makes 8 servings.

Tartar Sauce: In a small bowl stir together ½ cup *mayonnaise* or *salad dressing*, 1 tablespoon chopped *celery leaves*, 1 tablespoon *sweet* or *dill pickle relish*, 1 tablespoon *capers*, and 1 tablespoon chopped *white ends of green onions*.

Nutrition Facts per serving: 149 cal., 13 g total fat (2 g sat. fat), 60 mg chol., 280 mg sodium, 4 g carbo., 0 g fiber, 6 g pro.

Daily Values: 13% vit. A, 2% vit. C, 4% calcium, 3% iron

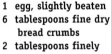

Brie Bundles

2/3 cup chutney
1 1/2 teaspoons snipped fresh rosemary or 1/2 teaspoon dried rosemary, crushed
1/4 cup toasted almonds, chopped
9 sheets (18×14 inches) frozen phyllo dough, thawed
1/2 cup butter or margarine, melted
1 4 1/2-ounce round Brie cheese, cut into 36 pieces

1 Snip any large pieces of chutney. In a small bowl combine chutney, rosemary, and almonds; set aside. Lightly brush 1 sheet of phyllo dough with some of the butter or margarine. Place a second phyllo sheet on top of the first; brush with some of the butter or margarine. Repeat with a third sheet of phyllo and more butter or margarine. (Cover remaining phyllo with plastic wrap to prevent it from drying out.) Cut the stack of phyllo into twelve 4-inch squares, trimming the edges as necessary.

2 Place a piece of Brie in the center of each phyllo square. Top with about 1 teaspoon of the chutney mixture. Bring the 4 corners of each phyllo square together. Pinch edges together to make a bundle; twist top slightly. Repeat with remaining phyllo dough, butter or margarine, Brie, and chutney mixture to make a total of 36 bundles.

3 Arrange bundles on an ungreased parchment- or foil-lined baking sheet. Bake, uncovered, in a 375° oven for 10 to 15 minutes or until golden brown. Serve warm. Makes 36 bundles.

Nutrition Facts per bundle: 70 cal., 4 g total fat (1 g sat. fat), 4 mg chol., 80 mg sodium, 7 g carbo., 0 g fiber, 1 g pro.
Daily Values: 7% vit. A, 4% vit. C, 1% calcium, 1% iron

Savory Stuffed Mushrooms

24 large fresh mushrooms (1 1/2 to 2 inches in diameter)
1 tablespoon olive oil
1/2 cup finely chopped cooked ham
1/4 cup crumbled blue cheese (1 ounce)
3 tablespoons fine dry bread crumbs
2 tablespoons snipped fresh parsley
2 tablespoons olive oil
2 cloves garlic, minced
1/8 teaspoon ground red pepper

1 Wash and drain mushrooms. Remove stems and save for another use. Lightly brush rounded side of the mushroom caps with the 1 tablespoon olive oil. Place mushrooms, cavity sides up, in a 13×9×2-inch baking pan; set aside.

2 Combine ham, blue cheese, fine dry bread crumbs, parsley, the 2 tablespoons olive oil, garlic, and red pepper. Spoon ham mixture into mushroom caps. Cover and chill for 2 to 24 hours.

3 Bake, uncovered, in a 425° oven for 15 to 17 minutes or until mushrooms are tender and filling is hot. Makes 24 appetizers.

Nutrition Facts per appetizer: 32 cal., 3 g total fat (1 g sat. fat), 3 mg chol., 78 mg sodium, 1 g carbo., 0 g fiber, 2 g pro.
Daily Values: 1% vit. A, 1% vit. C, 1% calcium, 1% iron

Green Chile-Chicken Meatballs

1 medium onion, finely chopped (1/2 cup)
1 large tart green apple, peeled, cored, and finely chopped
2 teaspoons cooking oil
3/4 cup soft bread crumbs (about 1 slice)
1 4-ounce can diced green chile peppers, drained (1/3 cup)
2 tablespoons frozen apple juice concentrate, thawed
1 egg white, slightly beaten
1/4 teaspoon ground cinnamon
1/4 teaspoon ground cumin
1/4 teaspoon dried marjoram, crushed
1/2 pound ground chicken or turkey
1/2 pound lean ground pork
Honey-Mustard sauce

 In a medium skillet cook onion and apple in oil over medium heat about 5 minutes or until tender. In a medium bowl combine onion mixture, bread crumbs, chile peppers, apple juice concentrate, egg white, 1/2 teaspoon *salt,* cinnamon, cumin, and marjoram. Mix in ground chicken or turkey and pork until combined. Form into thirty-six 1-inch meatballs.

Arrange meatballs in a 15×10×1-inch baking pan. Bake, uncovered, in a 350° oven for 15 to 20 minutes or until no pink remains. Toss with Honey-Mustard Sauce. Makes 36 meatballs.

Honey-Mustard Sauce: In a small saucepan combine 1/3 cup *honey,* 3 tablespoons *Dijon-style mustard,* 2 tablespoons finely chopped *onion,* 2 tablespoons *apple cider* or *apple juice,* and 1/8 teaspoon *ground red pepper.* Heat to boiling; reduce heat and boil gently, uncovered, for 7 minutes or until onion is tender and sauce is slightly thickened.

Nutrition Facts per meatball: 39 cal., 1 g total fat (0 g sat. fat), 3 mg chol., 52 mg sodium, 5 g carbo., 0 g fiber, 2 g pro.
Daily Values: 1% vit. A, 11% vit. C, 1% calcium, 1% iron

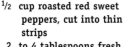

Macho Nachos

5 7- or 8-inch corn or flour tortillas or 4 cups tortilla chips (about 4 ounces)
1 cup canned black beans, drained and rinsed
1/2 cup salsa
2 cups shredded Monterey Jack, cheddar, queso quesadilla, Chihuahua, and/or asadero cheese (8 ounces)
1/2 cup roasted red sweet peppers, cut into thin strips
2 to 4 tablespoons fresh or canned sliced jalapeño peppers, drained (see Note, page 23)

 For tortilla chips, stack tortillas and cut into wedges with scissors or a sharp knife. Place wedges in a single layer on an ungreased baking sheet. Bake in a 350° oven for 10 to 12 minutes or until light golden brown. Remove the chips from oven. On an 11- or 12-inch oven-proof platter arrange tortilla chips in a single layer, overlapping slightly.

In a saucepan combine black beans and salsa; cook and stir over medium heat just until heated through. Remove from heat; spoon bean mixture over chips.

Sprinkle cheese, sweet peppers, and jalapeño peppers over bean mixture on chips. Bake in a 425° oven for 3 to 5 minutes or until cheese is melted. Serve immediately. Makes 10 servings.

Nutrition Facts per serving: 148 cal., 7 g total fat (4 g sat. fat), 20 mg chol., 220 mg sodium, 14 g carbo., 2 g fiber, 9 g pro.
Daily Values: 5% vit. A, 37% vit. C, 20% calcium, 8% iron

Salmon and Eggs in Puff Pastry
(recipe, page 28)

Breakfast & Brunch

Crisp temperatures and bright sunshine wake up our appetites. Morning is a fun time to get together for good company, fresh coffee, and a hearty meal. Best of all, preparation for most of these breakfast and brunch recipes can be done the day before. They'll go from refrigerator to oven or table so the hosts don't have to rise at dawn to begin cooking.

Salmon and Eggs in Puff Pastry

½ of a 17¼-ounce package frozen puff pastry (1 sheet)
8 eggs
½ cup fat-free milk
¼ teaspoon salt
¼ teaspoon black pepper
1 tablespoon butter or margarine
½ of an 8-ounce tub cream cheese with chive and onion
½ teaspoon dried dillweed
3 ounces thinly sliced smoked salmon (lox-style)
⅓ cup shredded mozzarella cheese (1½ ounces)
1 egg, slightly beaten
1 tablespoon water
Puff Pastry Stars (optional)

1 Thaw puff pastry according to package directions. Lightly grease a baking sheet; set aside. In a mixing bowl beat together 8 eggs, milk, salt, and black pepper. In a large skillet melt butter or margarine over medium heat; pour in egg mixture. Cook without stirring until mixture begins to set on the bottom and around edge.

2 Using a spatula or a large spoon, lift and fold the partially cooked eggs so the uncooked portion flows underneath. Continue cooking over medium heat for 2 minutes or until eggs are just set. Remove from heat; dot with cream cheese and sprinkle with dillweed. Stir gently until combined. Set aside.

3 Unfold pastry on a lightly floured surface; roll into a 17×12-inch rectangle. Place on a baking sheet (short sides may extend over sides of sheet). Arrange the smoked salmon crosswise down the center one-third of the pastry to within 1 inch of the top and bottom edges of the pastry. Spoon scrambled eggs over salmon.

4 Sprinkle eggs with the mozzarella cheese. Combine beaten egg and water. Brush the edges of the pastry with the egg mixture. Fold one short side of the pastry over the filling.

5 Fold the remaining short side over top. Seal top and ends well and brush the top of the pastry with the egg mixture. If desired, top with about 10 to 12 Puff Pastry Stars and brush with egg mixture.

6 Bake in a 375° oven for 25 minutes or until pastry is golden brown. (Or, if desired, cover and chill unbaked pastry for up to 24 hours. Uncover; bake in a 375° oven for 35 to 40 minutes or until pastry is golden brown and filling is hot.) Makes 6 servings.

Puff Pastry Stars: Thaw the remaining sheet of *puff pastry* and unfold it on a lightly floured surface. Roll the pastry into a 10-inch square. Using a 1-inch star-shaped cutter, cut out stars. Place 10 to 12 stars on the unbaked pastry. Place remaining star cutouts on an ungreased baking sheet; bake in a 375° oven for 12 to 15 minutes or until golden. Makes about 40 cutouts.

Nutrition Facts per serving: 417 cal., 30 g total fat (7 g sat. fat), 347 mg chol., 580 mg sodium, 18 g carbo., 0 g fiber, 17 g pro.
Daily Values: 23% vit. A, 1% vit. C, 10% calcium, 8% iron

Apricot-Apple Sipper

4 cups apple cider or apple juice
4 cups apricot nectar
2 tablespoons lemon juice
2 tablespoons honey
1 teaspoon whole cloves
1 teaspoon whole allspice
4 inches stick cinnamon, broken
Fresh strawberries (optional)

1 In a large saucepan combine apple cider or juice, apricot nectar, lemon juice, and honey. For spice bag, place cloves, allspice, and stick cinnamon on a double-thick, 6-inch square of 100-percent-cotton cheesecloth. Bring corners together and tie with a clean string. Add the spice bag to cider or juice mixture.

2 Bring the mixture to boiling; reduce heat. Cover and simmer for 10 minutes. Discard spice bag. Cool the mixture and chill in the refrigerator for several hours.

3 Serve chilled mixture in glasses. If desired, garnish each drink with a fresh strawberry. Makes 10 (6-ounce) servings.

Nutrition Facts per serving: 120 cal., 0 g total fat, 0 mg chol., 6 mg sodium, 32 g carbo., 1 g fiber, 0 g pro.
Daily Values: 13% vit. A, 59% vit. C, 1% calcium, 5% iron

Raspberry Tea

2 cups fresh or frozen red raspberries
4 or 5 tea bags
5 cups boiling water
Ice cubes

1 Place raspberries and tea bags in a glass bowl. Pour boiling water over raspberries and tea bags. Cover; let stand 5 minutes. Remove bags. Strain berries from mixture; discard berries. Cover and chill several hours in refrigerator. Serve over ice cubes. Makes 6 (6-ounce) servings.

Nutrition Facts per serving: 12 cal., 0 g total fat, 0 mg chol., 6 mg sodium, 3 g carbo., 1 g fiber, 0 g pro.
Daily Values: 8% vit. C, 1% iron

Eggnog Latte

2 cups dairy or canned eggnog
1 tablespoon light-colored rum
1 tablespoon bourbon
1 cup hot brewed espresso
Ground nutmeg

1 In a small heavy saucepan heat eggnog over medium heat until hot (do not boil). Stir rum and bourbon into hot espresso.

2 Transfer about half the eggnog and half the espresso mixture to a blender container. Cover; blend until very frothy. Repeat with remaining mixtures.

3 Divide evenly among coffee cups. Sprinkle with nutmeg. Makes 5 (6- to 8-ounce) servings.

Nutrition Facts per serving: 142 cal., 7 g total fat (0 g sat. fat), 0 mg chol., 65 mg sodium, 13 g carbo., 0 g fiber, 2 g pro.
Daily Values: 6% calcium

Ginger-Marinated Fruit

Ginger-Marinated Fruit

½ cup water
4 teaspoons finely
   shredded orange peel
1 tablespoon sugar
1 teaspoon grated fresh
   ginger
½ cup orange liqueur or
   ½ cup orange juice
   plus 1 tablespoon
   sugar
⅓ cup orange juice
¼ cup honey
6 cups cut-up assorted
   fruit such as kiwi
   fruit, apples, oranges,
   cantaloupe, honeydew
   melon, pineapple,
   pears, and/or red
   seedless grapes
   Fresh mint (optional)

1 In a small saucepan combine water, orange peel, sugar, and ginger. Bring to boiling; reduce heat. Cover; simmer over low heat for 5 minutes. Remove saucepan from heat. Stir in liqueur, orange juice, and honey. Cool thoroughly.

2 Pour cooled ginger mixture over fruit. Cover and marinate fruit for at least 1 hour or up to 12 hours in the refrigerator. To serve, spoon fruit and marinade into individual dishes. If desired, garnish with fresh mint. Makes 8 to 10 servings.

Nutrition Facts per serving: 158 cal., 0 g total fat, 0 mg chol., 3 mg sodium, 38 g carbo.,
5 g fiber, 1 g pro.
Daily Values: 98% vit. C

Sunrise Fruit Compote

1 lemon
1 orange or tangerine
1 lime
⅓ cup sugar
2 large pears, cored and
   sliced
2 medium papayas,
   peeled, seeded, and
   cubed
1 cup seedless red grapes
   Fresh mint (optional)

1 Halve lemon, orange or tangerine, and lime; squeeze out all of the juices (about ¾ cup total); reserve citrus shells. In a small saucepan bring the juices, sugar, and half of the citrus shells to boiling. Cook and stir until sugar is dissolved. Reduce heat and simmer, uncovered, for 5 minutes. Carefully remove shells; discard.

2 Place pears, papayas, and grapes in a large bowl. Pour hot syrup over fruit, gently stirring to mix. Cover and chill up to 4 hours. If desired, garnish with mint. Makes 6 servings.

Nutrition Facts per serving: 195 cal., 0 g total fat, 0 mg chol., 11 mg sodium,
49 g carbo., 5 g fiber, 1 g pro.
Daily Values: 202% vit. C

Mexicali Potato Brunch Bake

3 cups refrigerated shredded hash brown potatoes
5 eggs
1 cup shredded Monterey Jack cheese with jalapeño peppers (4 ounces)
½ cup ricotta cheese or cream cheese, softened
¾ cup milk, half-and-half, or light cream
⅛ teaspoon salt
⅛ teaspoon black pepper
2 tablespoons butter or margarine
1 tablespoon all-purpose flour
1 4-ounce can diced green chile peppers

1 Stir together the potatoes, 1 egg, and ½ cup of the shredded cheese. Spread mixture into bottom of a greased 2-quart square baking dish. Spread with a thin layer of ricotta or cream cheese.

2 Beat together remaining eggs, ¼ cup of the milk, salt, and black pepper. In a medium skillet melt 1 tablespoon of the butter or margarine over medium heat; add egg mixture. Cook, without stirring, until mixture begins to set on the bottom and around edge. Using a spatula or a large spoon, lift and fold partially cooked egg mixture so the uncooked portion flows underneath. Continue cooking about 4 minutes or until eggs are cooked through, but are still glossy and moist. Spoon eggs evenly over mixture in dish.

3 In same skillet melt remaining butter or margarine; stir in flour. Add remaining milk and the chile peppers; cook and stir until thickened and bubbly. Stir in remaining cheese until melted. Spoon evenly over the eggs. Bake, uncovered, in a 375° oven 25 minutes. Makes 6 servings.

Nutrition Facts per serving: 289 cal., 16 g total fat (7 g sat. fat), 203 mg chol., 406 mg sodium, 22 g carbo., 2 g fiber, 16 g pro.
Daily Values: 22% vit. A, 143% vit. C, 23% calcium, 8% iron

Brunch Turnovers

1 17¼-ounce package (2 sheets) frozen puff pastry
2 tablespoons finely chopped onion
1 tablespoon butter or margarine
1 egg, beaten
1 cup shredded Swiss cheese (4 ounces)
⅔ cup finely chopped cooked ham (3 ounces)
1 tablespoon snipped fresh parsley
½ teaspoon dried dillweed or 1 teaspoon snipped fresh dill
Dash garlic powder
Dash black pepper

1 Let frozen puff pastry stand at room temperature about 1 hour or until thawed. In a small saucepan cook onion in hot butter or margarine until tender. For filling, in a medium bowl combine egg, Swiss cheese, ham, parsley, dillweed, garlic powder, and black pepper. Stir in onion mixture; set aside.

2 On a lightly floured surface, roll each pastry sheet slightly into a 10½-inch square; cut into 3½-inch squares (18 total). Place 1 packed tablespoon of the filling just off center on each square. Moisten edges with water; fold in half diagonally. Seal edges by pressing with tines of a fork or your fingers. Place turnovers on an ungreased baking sheet.

3 Bake turnovers in a 400° oven about 25 minutes or until golden brown. Serve hot. Makes 18 turnovers.

Nutrition Facts per turnover: 162 cal., 12 g total fat (1 g sat. fat), 20 mg chol., 195 mg sodium, 10 g carbo., 0 g fiber, 4 g pro.
Daily Values: 3% vit. A, 1% vit. C, 6% calcium, 1% iron

Turkey Enchiladas

½ cup chopped onion
½ of an 8-ounce package reduced-fat cream cheese (Neufchâtel), softened
1 tablespoon water
1 teaspoon ground cumin
⅛ teaspoon black pepper
⅛ teaspoon salt
4 cups chopped cooked turkey or chicken breast
¼ cup chopped pecans, toasted
12 7- to 8-inch flour tortillas
Nonstick cooking spray
1 10¾-ounce can reduced-sodium condensed cream of chicken soup
1 8-ounce carton light dairy sour cream
1 cup fat-free milk
2 to 4 tablespoons finely chopped pickled jalapeño peppers
½ cup shredded reduced-fat sharp cheddar cheese (2 ounces)
Snipped fresh cilantro or parsley (optional)
Chopped tomatoes (optional)
Chopped sweet pepper (optional)

1 In a small saucepan cook onion, covered, in a small amount of boiling water over medium heat until tender; drain. In a medium bowl stir together cream cheese, water, cumin, black pepper, and salt. Stir in cooked onion, turkey, and pecans. Stack tortillas; wrap in foil. Heat in a 350° oven for 10 to 15 minutes to soften.

2 Meanwhile, coat a 3-quart rectangular baking dish with nonstick spray. For each enchilada, spoon about ¼ cup of the turkey mixture onto a tortilla; roll up. Place tortilla, seam side down, in the baking dish. Repeat with remaining filling and tortillas.

3 For sauce, in a medium bowl stir together soup, sour cream, milk, and jalapeño peppers; pour mixture over enchiladas. Bake, covered, in a 350° oven about 40 minutes or until heated through. Sprinkle enchiladas with the shredded cheddar cheese. Bake enchiladas, uncovered, for 4 to 5 minutes more or until the cheese is melted. If desired, top with snipped fresh cilantro or parsley, chopped tomatoes, and chopped sweet pepper. Makes 12 servings.

Nutrition Facts per serving: 272 cal., 10 g total fat (3 g sat. fat), 57 mg chol., 398 mg sodium, 22 g carbo., 1 g fiber, 22 g pro.
Daily Values: 1% vit. C, 11% calcium, 13% iron

Citrus-Mint Kiss

Christmas Morning Strata

Christmas Morning Strata

1 cup broccoli florets
5 cups ½-inch French
   bread cubes
   (about 8 ounces)
2 cups shredded cheddar
   cheese (8 ounces)
1 cup cubed cooked ham
   (6 ounces)
3 eggs, beaten
1¾ cups milk
2 tablespoons finely
   chopped onion
1 teaspoon dry mustard
   Dash black pepper

1 In a small saucepan cook broccoli, covered, in a small amount of boiling water for 4 to 6 minutes or until just tender; drain well. Set aside.

2 In a greased 2-quart square baking dish layer half of the bread cubes. Top with cheese, ham, and broccoli. Top with the remaining bread cubes. In a mixing bowl, combine the beaten eggs, milk, onion, mustard, and pepper. Pour egg mixture evenly over the layers in dish. Cover and chill in the refrigerator for 2 to 24 hours.

3 Uncover and bake in a 325° oven for 1 hour or until a knife inserted near the center comes out clean. Let stand about 5 minutes before serving. Makes 6 servings.

Nutrition Facts per serving: 377 cal., 20 g total fat (11 g sat. fat), 165 mg chol., 886 mg sodium, 25 g carbo., 2 g fiber, 24 g pro.
Daily Values: 18% vit. A, 21% vit. C, 41% calcium, 12% iron

Citrus-Mint Kiss

1 cup snipped fresh mint
   leaves
2 cups water
⅔ cup sugar
1 teaspoon shredded
   orange peel
2 cups orange juice
⅔ cup lemon juice
   Cracked ice
   Fresh mint sprigs
   (optional)

1 Place mint leaves in a medium bowl. In a small saucepan bring water and sugar to boiling, stirring until sugar dissolves. Remove from heat; pour over mint leaves. Stir in orange peel, orange juice, and lemon juice. Cover; let stand at room temperature for 1 hour. Strain. Cover and chill. Serve over ice. If desired, garnish with mint sprigs. Makes 6 (4-ounce) servings.

Nutrition Facts per serving: 95 cal., 0 g total fat, 0 mg chol., 3 mg sodium, 24 g carbo., 0 g fiber, 1 g pro.
Daily Values: 3% vit. A, 68% vit. C, 1% calcium, 1% iron

Stuffed French Toast

1 8-ounce package cream
   cheese, softened
1 12-ounce jar apricot
   preserves
   (about 1 cup)
1 teaspoon vanilla
1/2 cup chopped walnuts
1 16-ounce loaf French
   bread
4 eggs
1 cup whipping cream
1/2 teaspoon ground
   nutmeg
1/2 teaspoon vanilla
1/2 cup orange juice

1 In a small mixing bowl beat together cream cheese, 2 tablespoons of the apricot preserves, and the 1 teaspoon vanilla until fluffy. Stir in nuts; set aside. Cut bread into ten to twelve 1½-inch-thick slices; cut a pocket in the top-crust edge of each. Fill each pocket with about 1½ tablespoons of the cream cheese mixture.

2 Beat together eggs, whipping cream, nutmeg, and the ½ teaspoon vanilla. Using tongs, dip the filled bread slices in the egg mixture, being careful not to squeeze out the filling. Cook on a lightly greased griddle over medium heat about 2 minutes on each side or until golden brown. Keep warm in 300° oven while cooking remaining slices.

3 Meanwhile, in a small saucepan heat together the remaining apricot preserves and the orange juice. To serve, drizzle the apricot preserves mixture over hot French toast. Makes 10 to 12 slices.

Nutrition Facts per slice: 456 cal., 24 g total fat (12 g sat. fat), 143 mg chol., 383 mg sodium, 52 g carbo., 1 g fiber, 10 g pro.
Daily Values: 15% vit. A, 12% vit. C, 9% calcium, 15% iron

Sausage-Potato Lasagna

1/2 pound bulk Italian
   sausage
2 cups sliced fresh
   mushrooms
   (about 6 ounces)
4 medium potatoes,
   peeled and thinly
   sliced
1 egg, beaten
1½ cups ricotta cheese
1/4 cup grated Parmesan or
   Romano cheese
1 10-ounce package
   frozen chopped
   spinach, thawed and
   well drained
1 medium onion,
   chopped (1/2 cup)
2 cloves garlic, minced
2 tablespoons butter or
   margarine
2 tablespoons all-purpose
   flour
1/4 teaspoon ground
   nutmeg
1½ cups milk
1 cup shredded
   mozzarella cheese
   (4 ounces)

1 In a large skillet cook sausage and mushrooms over medium-high heat until meat is brown. Drain off fat.

2 In a large covered saucepan cook sliced potatoes in boiling water for 5 minutes (they won't be thoroughly cooked). Drain; set aside.

3 For filling, stir together the egg, ricotta cheese, Parmesan or Romano cheese, and spinach; set aside.

4 For sauce, in a medium saucepan cook onion and garlic in hot butter or margarine until onion is tender. Stir in flour and nutmeg. Add milk all at once. Cook and stir until thickened and bubbly.

5 Layer half of the potatoes in a greased 2-quart rectangular baking dish. Top with half of the spinach mixture. Top with half of the meat mixture, half of the sauce, and half of the mozzarella cheese. Repeat layers, except reserve remaining cheese.

6 Cover with foil and bake in a 350° oven about 35 minutes or until potatoes are tender. Uncover; sprinkle with reserved cheese and bake 5 minutes more or until cheese is melted. Let stand for 10 minutes before serving. Makes 6 to 8 servings.

Nutrition Facts per serving: 436 cal., 22 g total fat (10 g sat. fat), 95 mg chol., 616 mg sodium, 34 g carbo., 2 g fiber, 26 g pro.
Daily Values: 46% vit. A, 23% vit. C, 41% calcium, 15% iron

Monkey Bread Rolls

1 35-ounce package
    frozen cinnamon sweet
    roll dough or frozen
    orange sweet roll
    dough (12 rolls)
2/3 cup chopped pecans
1/3 cup butter or
    margarine, melted
1 cup sugar
1/3 cup caramel ice cream
    topping
1 tablespoon maple-
    flavored syrup

1 The night before brunch, place frozen rolls about 2 inches apart on a large greased cookie sheet. Cover with plastic wrap. Refrigerate overnight to let dough thaw and begin to rise.

2 Generously grease eight 3¼-inch muffin cups or eight 10-ounce custard cups. Sprinkle ⅓ cup of the pecans in the bottoms of the cups.

3 Cut each roll in half with a table knife. Dip each half roll into melted butter or margarine, then roll in sugar. Stack 3 of the halves in each prepared muffin or custard cup. Drizzle with any remaining butter or margarine; sprinkle with any remaining sugar. Sprinkle the remaining ⅓ cup pecans on top.

4 Combine ice cream topping and maple-flavored syrup; drizzle over top. Place muffin tin or custard cups on a large baking sheet. Bake in a 350° oven about 25 minutes or until golden brown. Let stand 1 minute. Invert onto individual plates or large serving platter. Spoon any topping and nuts that remain in cups or pan onto rolls. Cool slightly. Serve warm. Makes 8 large rolls.

Nutrition Facts per roll: 682 cal., 26 g total fat (2 g sat. fat), 0 mg chol., 550 mg sodium, 109 g carbo., 3 g fiber, 8 g pro.
Daily Values: 7% vit. A, 7% calcium, 17% iron

Raspberry-Cheese Coffee Cake

1 8-ounce package cream
    cheese, softened
1/2 cup butter or
    margarine
1 3/4 cups all-purpose flour
1 cup granulated sugar
2 eggs
1/4 cup milk
1 teaspoon baking
    powder
1/2 teaspoon baking soda
1/2 teaspoon vanilla
1/2 cup seedless red
    raspberry preserves or
    strawberry preserves
    Powdered sugar

1 Grease a 13×9×2-inch baking pan; set aside. In a large mixing bowl beat cream cheese and butter or margarine with an electric mixer on medium to high speed about 30 seconds or until combined. Add about half of the flour to the cream cheese mixture.

2 Add the granulated sugar, eggs, milk, baking powder, baking soda, and vanilla to cream cheese mixture. Beat on low speed until thoroughly combined, scraping the side of bowl. Beat on medium speed for 2 minutes. Beat in remaining flour on low speed just until combined.

3 Spread batter evenly into prepared pan. Spoon preserves in small mounds on top of the batter. Using a small narrow spatula or knife, gently swirl preserves into the batter to create a marbled effect.

4 Bake in a 350° oven for 30 to 35 minutes or until a wooden toothpick inserted near the center comes out clean. Cool in the pan on wire rack for 15 minutes. Sift powdered sugar over coffee cake. Serve warm, or cool on wire rack. Makes 12 servings.

Nutrition Facts per serving: 317 cal., 16 g total fat (7 g sat. fat), 67 mg chol., 224 mg sodium, 40 g carbo., 1 g fiber, 4 g pro.
Daily Values: 17% vit. A, 5% calcium, 8% iron

Cinnamon-Orange Coffee Cake

Cinnamon-Orange Coffee Cake

4 to 4½ cups all-purpose flour

2 packages active dry yeast

½ cup milk

⅓ cup sugar

⅓ cup butter or margarine

1 teaspoon salt

2 eggs

½ cup orange juice

2 tablespoons finely shredded orange peel

3 tablespoons butter or margarine, melted

½ cup sugar

½ cup coconut (optional)

2 teaspoons ground cinnamon
  Orange Glaze

1 Stir together 2 cups of the flour and the yeast in a large bowl; set aside. Heat and stir milk, the ⅓ cup sugar, ⅓ cup butter or margarine, and salt in a medium saucepan until warm (120° to 130°) and butter or margarine almost melts. Add to flour mixture. Add eggs and orange juice. Beat with an electric mixer on low to medium speed for 30 seconds, scraping sides of bowl. Beat on high speed for 3 minutes. Using a wooden spoon, stir in orange peel and as much of the remaining flour as you can.

2 Turn dough out onto a lightly floured surface. Knead in enough of the remaining flour to make a moderately soft dough that is smooth and elastic (3 to 5 minutes). Shape dough into a ball. Place dough in a lightly greased bowl, turning once to grease surface. Cover and let rise in a warm place about 1½ hours or until double in size.

3 Punch dough down. Turn dough out onto a lightly floured surface. Divide the dough in half. Cover and let rest 10 minutes. Grease 2 baking sheets.

4 Roll each half of the dough into a 15×10-inch rectangle. Brush each dough rectangle with half of the melted butter or margarine. Combine the ½ cup sugar, coconut, if desired, and cinnamon. Sprinkle half of the sugar mixture over each dough rectangle.

5 Roll up each rectangle, starting from one of the long sides. Pinch seams to seal. Place seam side up on prepared baking sheets. Fold half of each roll over the top of its other half, sealing ends. Starting 1½ inches from the sealed end, cut all the way through the dough to the folded end. Turn cut sides out so they face up, forming a heart shape. Cover and let dough rise in a warm place about 30 minutes or until nearly double.

6 Bake in a 375° oven about 20 minutes or until lightly browned. Remove from baking sheets and place on wire racks. Let cool slightly. Drizzle with Orange Glaze. Serve warm or cool. Makes 2 coffee cakes, 12 servings each.

Orange Glaze: In a small bowl stir together 1 cup sifted *powdered sugar* and 1 teaspoon finely shredded *orange peel*. Stir in enough *orange juice* (1 to 2 tablespoons) to make a frosting of drizzling consistency.

Nutrition Facts per serving: 161 cal., 5 g total fat (3 g sat. fat), 29 mg chol., 137 mg sodium, 27 g carbo., 1 g fiber, 3 g pro.

Daily Values: 4% vit. A, 6% vit. C, 1% calcium, 7% iron

Fruited Baked Ham
(recipe, page 42)

Wild Rice-Stuffed Squash
(recipe, page 58)

Dinner Is Served

Gather around the table for a festive dinner with all the trimmings. Whether your family prefers a golden-brown turkey, a flavorful baked ham, or a succulent prime rib, in this chapter you'll find the perfect main course plus an abundance of delicious salads, vegetable side dishes, and breads to round out a memorable meal.

Fruited Baked Ham

1 3- to 4-pound fully
   cooked smoked
   boneless ham
½ cup apricot preserves
1 cup cherry preserves
¼ cup orange juice

1 Place ham in a shallow roasting pan. Score top in a diamond pattern. Insert meat thermometer. Roast, uncovered, in a 325° oven for 1½ to 2¼ hours or until thermometer registers 140°.

2 For sauce, snip any large pieces of apricot in the preserves. In a small saucepan warm apricot and cherry preserves and orange juice over low heat until heated through. Slice ham; serve with sauce. Makes 12 to 16 servings.

Nutrition Facts per serving: 315 cal., 10 g total fat (4 g sat. fat), 67 mg chol., 1,714 mg sodium, 28 g carbo., 0 g fiber, 26 g pro.
Daily Values: 10% vit. C, 2% calcium, 10% iron

Festive Pork Roast

1 5-pound boneless pork
   loin roast (rolled and
   tied)
1½ cups dry red wine
⅔ cup packed brown
   sugar
½ cup vinegar
½ cup catsup
½ cup water
¼ cup cooking oil
2 tablespoons soy sauce
2 cloves garlic, minced
2 teaspoons curry powder
1 teaspoon ground ginger
½ teaspoon black pepper
2 tablespoons cornstarch

1 Place roast in a large self-sealing plastic bag; set in a large, deep bowl. For marinade, in a small mixing bowl combine wine, brown sugar, vinegar, catsup, water, oil, soy sauce, garlic, curry powder, ginger, and black pepper. Pour marinade over meat; seal bag. Marinate in refrigerator for 6 to 8 hours or overnight, turning bag several times. Drain meat, reserving marinade in the refrigerator. Pat meat dry with paper towels.

2 Place the meat on a rack in a shallow roasting pan. Insert meat thermometer. Roast in a 325° oven for 2¼ to 2½ hours or until meat thermometer registers 155°.

3 About 25 minutes before the meat is done, make sauce. In a small saucepan stir cornstarch into reserved marinade. Cook and stir until thickened and bubbly. Cook 2 minutes more. Brush roast frequently with sauce during the last 15 minutes of roasting. Let meat stand, covered, about 15 minutes before slicing. (The meat temperature will rise 5° during standing.) Reheat remaining sauce and pass with meat. Makes 12 to 15 servings.

Nutrition Facts per serving: 344 cal., 17 g total fat (5 g sat. fat), 85 mg chol., 394 mg sodium, 16 g carbo., 0 g fiber, 27 g pro.
Daily Values: 1% vit. A, 4% vit. C, 1% calcium, 11% iron

Cranberry-Burgundy Glazed Ham

1 10- to 14-pound
   bone-in cooked ham
   Whole cloves
1 16-ounce can whole
   cranberry sauce
½ cup packed brown
   sugar
½ cup Burgundy or other
   dry red wine
1 tablespoon prepared
   mustard

1 Place the ham, fat side-up, on a rack in a shallow roasting pan. Score fat in diamond pattern; stud with whole cloves. Insert meat thermometer into thickest portion of ham without touching bone. Bake in 325° oven about 3 hours or until thermometer registers 140°.

2 Meanwhile, in a medium saucepan stir together the cranberry sauce, brown sugar, wine, and mustard. Bring to boiling; reduce heat. Simmer, uncovered, for 5 minutes. Spoon half of the sauce over ham during the last 30 minutes of roasting. Reheat remaining sauce and pass with ham. Makes 32 servings.

Nutrition Facts per serving: 187 cal., 5 g total fat (2 g sat. fat), 54 mg chol., 1,306 mg sodium, 8 g carbo., 0 g fiber, 24 g pro.
Daily Values: 40% vit. C, 6% iron

Apple Saucy Pork Roast

1 3½- to 4-pound
   boneless pork top loin
   roast (double loin,
   tied)
3 cloves garlic, cut into
   thin slices
1 teaspoon coarse salt or
   regular salt
1 teaspoon dried
   rosemary, crushed
½ teaspoon coarsely
   ground black pepper
3 medium apples, cored
   and cut into wedges
   (about 3 cups)
¼ cup packed brown
   sugar
¼ cup apple juice
2 tablespoons lemon
   juice
2 teaspoons dry mustard

1 Cut slits about ½ inch long and 1 inch deep in pork roast; insert a piece of garlic in each slit. Combine salt, rosemary, and black pepper; rub onto meat surface. Place roast on a rack in a shallow roasting pan. Insert a meat thermometer. Roast, uncovered, in a 325° oven for 1½ to 1¾ hours or until the meat thermometer reaches 145°. Spoon off any grease from roasting pan.

2 Combine the apples, brown sugar, apple juice, lemon juice, and dry mustard. Spoon apple mixture around roast. Roast, uncovered, for 30 to 45 minutes longer or until meat thermometer reaches 155° and meat juices are clear.

3 Transfer meat to a platter. Cover and let meat stand for 10 minutes before slicing. (The meat temperature will rise 5° during standing.) Remove the rack from the pan. Stir apple wedges into pan juices. If desired, use a slotted spoon to remove apple wedges, and pass juices. Makes 10 to 12 servings.

Nutrition Facts per serving: 237 cal., 11 g total fat (4 g sat. fat), 72 mg chol., 271 mg sodium, 12 g carbo., 1 g fiber, 23 g pro.
Daily Values: 7% vit. C, 1% calcium, 7% iron

Roast Turkey
with Bread Stuffing

Roast Turkey with Bread Stuffing

1 cup chopped celery
1 cup sliced fresh
   mushrooms or one
   4-ounce can sliced
   mushrooms, drained
   (optional)
$\frac{1}{2}$ cup chopped onion
   (1 medium)
$\frac{1}{3}$ cup butter or
   margarine
1 teaspoon poultry
   seasoning or ground
   sage
$\frac{1}{4}$ teaspoon black pepper
$\frac{1}{8}$ teaspoon salt
8 cups dry bread cubes
$\frac{1}{2}$ to $\frac{3}{4}$ cup chicken broth
   or water
1 10- to 12-pound turkey
   Cooking oil
   Giblet Gravy (recipe,
   page 46)

1 For stuffing, in a large skillet cook celery, fresh mushrooms, if using, and onion in butter or margarine until tender; remove from heat. Stir in poultry seasoning or sage, black pepper, and salt. Place dry bread cubes in a large mixing bowl; add onion mixture and, if using, canned mushrooms. Drizzle bread mixture with enough broth or water to moisten, tossing lightly.

2 Rinse turkey on the outside as well as inside the body and neck cavities; pat dry. Season body cavity with *salt*. Spoon some of the stuffing loosely into neck cavity. Pull the neck skin to the back; fasten with a skewer.

3 Lightly spoon more stuffing into the body cavity. Use no more than $\frac{3}{4}$ cup stuffing per pound of turkey. (Place any remaining stuffing in a casserole, cover, and chill. Bake stuffing alongside turkey for 30 to 45 minutes or until heated through.) Tuck the ends of the drumsticks under the band of skin across the tail. If the band of skin is not present, tie the drumsticks securely to the tail with 100-percent-cotton string. Twist wing tips under the back.

4 Place turkey, breast side up, on a rack in a shallow roasting pan. Brush with oil. Insert a meat thermometer into the center of one of the inside thigh muscles. The thermometer bulb should not touch the bone. Cover turkey loosely with foil.

5 Roast turkey in a 325° oven for $3\frac{1}{4}$ to $3\frac{1}{2}$ hours or until thermometer registers 180° to 185°, juices run clear, and the center of the stuffing registers at least 165°. After $2\frac{1}{2}$ hours, cut band of skin or string between drumsticks so thighs will cook evenly. When done, drumsticks will move easily in their sockets and their thickest parts will feel soft when pressed. Uncover the last 45 minutes of roasting.

6 Remove turkey from oven. Cover; let stand 15 to 20 minutes before carving. Use a spoon to remove stuffing from turkey; place in a serving bowl. Carve turkey. Serve with Giblet Gravy. Makes 12 to 14 servings.

Nutrition Facts per serving: 392 cal., 19 g total fat (5 g sat. fat), 121 mg chol., 343 mg sodium, 14 g carbo., 1 g fiber, 38 g pro.
Daily Values: 15% vit. A, 2% vit. C, 6% calcium, 23% iron

Giblet Gravy

4 ounces turkey giblets and neck
1 stalk celery with leaves, cut up
½ small onion, cut up
Pan drippings from roast turkey
¼ cup all-purpose flour
¼ teaspoon salt
⅛ teaspoon black pepper

1 Rinse giblets and neck. Refrigerate liver until needed. In a medium saucepan combine remaining giblets, neck, celery, onion, and enough lightly salted water to cover. Bring to boiling; reduce heat. Cover and simmer about 1 hour or until tender. Add liver; simmer 20 to 30 minutes more or until tender. Remove giblets and finely chop. Discard neck bones. Strain broth. Discard vegetables. Chill giblets and broth while poultry roasts.

2 Transfer roast turkey to a serving platter; pour pan drippings into a large measuring cup. Skim and reserve fat from drippings. Pour ¼ cup of the fat into the saucepan (discard remaining fat).

3 Stir in flour, salt, and black pepper. Add the reserved broth to the drippings in the measuring cup to equal 1½ cups; add all at once to flour mixture in the saucepan.

4 Cook and stir over medium heat until thickened and bubbly. Cook and stir for 1 minute more. Stir in chopped giblets. Heat through. Makes 2 cups (8 to 10 servings).

Nutrition Facts per serving: 97 cal., 7 g total fat (2 g sat. fat), 44 mg chol., 173 mg sodium, 4 g carbo., 0 g fiber, 4 g pro.
Daily Values: 16% vit. A, 1% vit. C, 6% iron

Rosemary-Orange Grilled Turkey

4 cups hickory wood chips (optional)
2 tablespoons butter or margarine, softened
2 tablespoons snipped fresh rosemary
2 tablespoons finely shredded orange peel
1 8- to 10-pound turkey
2 tablespoons cooking oil

1 If using wood chips, at least 1 hour before grilling, soak wood chips in enough water to cover. In a small bowl combine softened butter or margarine, rosemary, and orange peel; set aside.

2 Remove the neck and giblets from turkey. Slip your fingers between skin and meat to loosen turkey skin over breast area. Lift turkey skin and carefully spread butter mixture directly over turkey meat. Skewer the neck skin to the back. Twist wing tips under back. Tuck drumsticks under the band of skin across the tail or tie legs to tail with 100-percent-cotton string. Place turkey, breast side up, on a rack in a roasting pan. Insert a meat thermometer into the center of an inside thigh muscle without the thermometer touching bone. Brush turkey with oil.

3 Drain wood chips. For a charcoal grill, arrange medium-hot coals around edge of grill. Test for medium heat above center of grill. Sprinkle one-fourth of the wood chips over the coals. Place turkey in pan on the grill rack over center of grill. Cover; grill for 2½ to 3 hours or until thermometer registers 180°. Add more wood chips every 30 minutes. Makes 12 to 14 servings.

Nutrition Facts per serving: 307 cal., 17 g total fat (4 g sat. fat), 122 mg chol., 113 mg sodium, 0 g carbo., 0 g fiber, 37 g pro.
Daily Values: 11% vit. A, 2% vit. C, 3% calcium, 17% iron

Stuffed Turkey Breast

1 3-pound turkey half breast
2 slices white bread, torn into small pieces
⅓ cup balsamic vinegar
4 ounces uncooked Italian sausage, casing removed (if present)
4 ounces ground uncooked turkey or chicken
4 ounces ground veal
1 egg, beaten
¼ cup finely snipped parsley
½ teaspoon salt
¼ teaspoon ground white pepper
2 tablespoons olive oil
1 tablespoon butter or margarine
1 medium onion, sliced into half rings
1 bay leaf
2 whole cloves
1 ½-inch piece stick cinnamon
½ teaspoon whole black peppercorns
¾ cup dry red wine
½ cup balsamic vinegar
¼ cup red grape juice
1 tablespoon all-purpose flour
½ cup water

1 Remove bone and trim any excess fat from the turkey breast, leaving skin intact. Cut slits to butterfly the thicker portions of turkey breast, being sure not to cut through skin. Pound with meat mallet to flatten where necessary until it is approximately 12×10 inches and ½ inch thick.

2 In a small bowl soak the bread pieces in the ⅓ cup balsamic vinegar for 10 minutes. In a large mixing bowl combine Italian sausage, ground turkey or chicken, ground veal, beaten egg, parsley, salt, and white pepper. Add the vinegar-soaked bread and mix well. Mound the stuffing mixture down the center of the turkey piece. Carefully fold the sides and ends up and around the stuffing, and tie with kitchen string, maintaining a loaf shape.

3 Heat olive oil and butter in a heavy, deep, very large skillet or a Dutch oven. Add the onion slices; cook over medium-high heat for 2 minutes. Reduce heat to medium. Carefully add the stuffed turkey breast and cook, gently turning to brown all sides. Be careful not to overcook the turkey or break the skin.

4 Add bay leaf, cloves, cinnamon stick, peppercorns, wine, ½ cup balsamic vinegar, and grape juice. Bring to boiling. Reduce heat, cover, and simmer over low heat for 25 minutes, making sure the breast does not stick to the bottom of the pan. Carefully turn the breast over and simmer, covered, 25 minutes more. Carefully remove the turkey; let cool about 30 minutes before slicing.

5 For sauce, strain the cooking liquid, removing all the onions, herbs, and spices. Measure cooking liquid; if necessary, add water to equal ¾ cup. Return mixture to skillet. Combine flour and water. Slowly stir flour mixture into the cooking liquid. Cook and stir until thickened and bubbly; cook 1 minute more.

6 When turkey is cool enough to handle, remove all string. Cut the breast into ½- to ¾-inch slices. Carefully reassemble the turkey slices on a heated serving platter; pour sauce over top. Makes 8 servings.

Nutrition Facts per serving: 360 cal., 12 g total fat (4 g sat. fat), 146 mg chol., 356 mg sodium, 13 g carbo., 0 g fiber, 42 g pro.
Daily Values: 4% vit. A, 5% vit. C, 4% calcium, 14% iron

Prime Rib au Poivre

Peas and Onions with Dill Butter
(recipe, page 57)

Prime Rib au Poivre

1   6- to 8-pound beef rib
    roast
2   tablespoons Dijon-style
    mustard
2   tablespoons bottled
    minced garlic or
    4 cloves garlic, minced
2   tablespoons whole
    black peppercorns,
    coarsely cracked

1   Have butcher completely loosen bones for easier carving of roast. Trim any excess fat from top of beef, leaving a layer about ¼ inch thick. Combine mustard and garlic; spread over top of beef. Sprinkle peppercorns over mustard mixture.

2   Place meat, bone side down, in a foil-lined shallow roasting pan. Insert a meat thermometer into center of meat without touching bone. Roast in a 350° oven until thermometer reaches 140° for medium rare (2¼ to 2½ hours) and 155° for medium (2¾ to 3 hours). Cover meat with foil. Let meat stand 15 minutes before carving. (The meat temperature will rise 5° during standing.) Makes 12 servings.

Nutrition Facts per serving: 487 cal., 40 g total fat (17 g sat. fat), 114 mg chol., 145 mg sodium, 1 g carbo., 0 g fiber, 29 g pro.
Daily Values: 2% vit. C, 1% calcium, 20% iron

Roast Beef with Mushroom Sauce

1   2- to 3-pound beef eye
    of round roast
2   tablespoons Dijon-style
    mustard
½   teaspoon coarsely
    ground black pepper
3   cups quartered fresh
    mushrooms
4   green onions, bias-
    sliced into ½-inch
    pieces
1   clove garlic, minced
2   tablespoons butter or
    margarine
¼   cup all-purpose flour
½   teaspoon dried thyme
    or marjoram, crushed
1½ cups beef broth
¼   cup light cream or milk

1   Trim fat from meat. Mix mustard and pepper; rub onto meat. Place meat on a rack in a shallow roasting pan. Insert a meat thermometer. Roast in a 325° oven until thermometer registers 140° for medium rare (1½ to 2 hours) or 155° for medium (1¾ to 2¼ hours). Cover with foil; let stand 15 minutes before carving. (The meat temperature will rise 5° during standing.)

2   Meanwhile, for sauce, in a medium saucepan cook mushrooms, green onions, and garlic in hot butter or margarine until green onions are tender. Stir in flour and thyme. Gradually stir in beef broth. Cook and stir over medium heat until thickened and bubbly. Cook and stir for 1 minute more. Stir in light cream or milk. Cook and stir until heated through.

3   Thinly slice meat across the grain. Arrange on a platter. Pour some sauce on meat. Pass remaining sauce. Makes 8 to 10 servings.

Nutrition Facts per serving: 229 cal., 10 g total fat (3 g sat. fat), 75 mg chol., 331 mg sodium, 5 g carbo., 1 g fiber, 29 g pro.
Daily Values: 5% vit. A, 4% vit. C, 1% calcium, 22% iron

Three-Way Mashed Potatoes

1½ pounds russet (baking)
    potatoes
  1 teaspoon salt
  2 tablespoons butter or
    margarine, softened
¼ teaspoon black pepper
⅓ cup milk, half-and-half,
    or light cream, warmed
⅓ cup dairy sour cream

1 Peel the potatoes in a random fashion, leaving about half the skin on each potato. Cut potatoes into large chunks and place in a large saucepan. Add cold water to cover along with ½ teaspoon of the salt. Bring to boiling; reduce heat. Cover and cook for 15 to 20 minutes or until potatoes are tender. Drain.

2 Add the butter or margarine, pepper, and the remaining ½ teaspoon salt to potatoes in saucepan. Using a potato masher, mash potatoes slightly, leaving some lumps, if desired. Gently mash in milk, about half at a time, then mash in the sour cream. With a wooden spoon, stir until potatoes are evenly mixed. Season to taste with additional salt and pepper, if desired. Serve at once. Makes 6 servings.

Nutrition Facts per serving: 148 cal., 7 g total fat (2 g sat. fat), 6 mg chol., 445 mg sodium, 19 g carbo., 2 g fiber, 4 g pro.

Daily Values: 7% vit. A, 26% vit. C, 4% calcium, 5% iron

Roasted Garlic Mashed Potatoes: Rub most of the papery skin off a head of *garlic*. With a sharp knife, slice off top third of the head of garlic. Put garlic in a small baking dish or custard cup and drizzle with about 1 tablespoon *olive oil*. Cover with foil. Bake in a 350° oven for 20 to 25 minutes or until garlic is very tender. Squeeze the roasted garlic cloves into a small bowl and mash with 1 tablespoon of the softened butter or margarine. Prepare the potatoes as directed, except add the garlic-butter mixture to potatoes along with the sour cream.

Parmesan-Basil Mashed Potatoes: Prepare the potatoes as directed, except after adding milk, add ½ cup finely shredded *Parmesan cheese* and 1 tablespoon finely snipped *fresh basil*. Add sour cream. Top mashed potatoes with additional finely shredded Parmesan cheese.

Sautéed Spinach Mashed Potatoes: Prepare the potatoes as directed, decreasing the warmed milk to ¼ cup. While potatoes are cooking, coarsely chop half of a 6-ounce package *baby spinach*. In a large skillet cook ⅓ cup chopped *onion* in 1 tablespoon *olive oil* for 5 minutes or until onion is tender. Stir in the spinach. Cook for 1 to 2 minutes or just until spinach wilts; stir the spinach mixture into the mashed potatoes. Add a dash of *grated nutmeg*, if desired.

Note: To keep mashed potatoes warm, transfer the prepared potatoes to a heat-proof serving bowl. Smooth top; pour 3 to 4 tablespoons of additional warmed milk or cream over potatoes to barely cover the surface. Cover the bowl with foil and place over a saucepan partially filled with hot water. Hold the bowl over low heat for up to 20 minutes. When ready to serve, stir in the milk to moisten potatoes.

Company Scalloped Potatoes

1 large onion, chopped
  (1 cup)
1 medium red and/or
  green sweet pepper,
  chopped (³/4 cup)
4 cloves garlic, minced
2 tablespoons butter or
  margarine
2 10³/4-ounce cans
  condensed cream of
  celery soup
2 cups milk
¹/4 teaspoon black pepper
8 cups sliced, peeled
  potatoes (about
  2³/4 pounds)
²/3 cup grated Parmesan
  cheese
1 cup soft bread crumbs
3 tablespoons butter or
  margarine, melted

1 In a large saucepan cook onion, sweet pepper, and garlic in 2 tablespoons butter or margarine about 5 minutes or until tender. Stir in soup, milk, and black pepper. Heat, stirring occasionally, until bubbly.

2 Layer half of the potatoes in a greased 3-quart oval or rectangular baking dish. Cover with half of the soup mixture. Sprinkle with half of the Parmesan cheese. Layer remaining potatoes and soup mixture. Cover dish with foil.

3 Bake in a 325° oven for 1½ hours or until nearly tender. Uncover and sprinkle with a mixture of bread crumbs, the remaining Parmesan cheese, and melted butter. Bake for 15 minutes more or until potatoes are tender and crumbs are golden. Let stand 15 minutes before serving. Makes 12 servings.

Nutrition Facts per serving: 232 cal., 10 g total fat (5 g sat. fat), 26 mg chol., 590 mg sodium, 30 g carbo., 2 g fiber, 7 g pro.
Daily Values: 11% vit. A, 22% vit. C, 13% calcium, 5% iron

Roasted Potatoes with Sage

2 pounds small Yukon
  Gold potatoes
¹/3 cup snipped fresh sage
4 teaspoons finely
  shredded lemon peel
2 tablespoons olive oil
1 tablespoon water
2 large cloves garlic,
  minced
1 teaspoon dried whole,
  mixed peppercorns,
  crushed
¹/2 teaspoon salt

1 In a large saucepan cook potatoes in boiling water for 10 minutes or until easily pierced by a knife but still firm. Meanwhile, combine sage, lemon peel, olive oil, water, garlic, peppercorns, and salt.

2 Drain potatoes and rinse with cold water. While still warm, cut potatoes into quarters. Lightly coat a 3-quart rectangular baking dish with *olive oil*. Place potatoes in dish. Pour the sage mixture over, and stir gently until potatoes are evenly coated.

3 Bake in 400° oven for 35 to 45 minutes until golden and crisp, stirring once halfway through baking. Serve at once. Makes 6 to 8 servings.

Nutrition Facts per serving: 190 cal., 5 g total fat (1 g sat. fat), 189 mg sodium, 34 g carbo., 2 g fiber, 4 g pro.
Daily Values: 36% vit. C, 32% calcium, 17% iron

Christmas Eve Salad

Christmas Eve Salad

¹/₃ cup olive oil
3 tablespoons vinegar
2 tablespoons lime juice
2 tablespoons sugar
2 medium oranges
2 cups cubed fresh
 pineapple or one
 20-ounce can juice-
 packed pineapple
 chunks, drained
1 large apple, cored and
 sliced
 Romaine leaves
4 cups shredded leaf
 lettuce
1 medium banana, sliced
1 16-ounce can sliced
 beets, rinsed and
 drained
1 cup jicama cut into
 thin bite-size strips
¹/₂ cup pine nuts or
 peanuts
¹/₂ cup finely chopped red
 onion or pomegranate
 seeds

1 For dressing, in a screw-top jar combine olive oil, vinegar, lime juice, and sugar. Cover and shake well. Chill for 2 to 24 hours.

2 Peel and section the oranges over a large mixing bowl to catch the juice. Add orange sections, pineapple, and apple slices to the bowl. Toss to coat all of the fruit with orange juice. Cover and chill for 2 to 24 hours.

3 To serve, line a serving platter with romaine leaves. Top with shredded lettuce. Add banana slices to the fruit mixture; toss to coat bananas with juice. Drain the fruit mixture. Arrange the fruit mixture, beets, and jicama on the platter. Sprinkle with pine nuts or peanuts and onion or pomegranate seeds. Shake the salad dressing and pour over salad. Makes 6 side-dish servings.

Nutrition Facts per serving: 303 cal., 19 g total fat (3 g sat. fat), 0 mg chol., 176 mg sodium, 34 g carbo., 4 g fiber, 6 g pro.
Daily Values: 12% vit. A, 83% vit. C, 5% calcium, 19% iron

Berry Salad

1 10-ounce package
 frozen sliced
 strawberries, thawed
1 10-ounce package
 frozen red raspberries,
 thawed
1 6-ounce package
 strawberry- or
 raspberry-flavored
 gelatin
1¹/₄ cups boiling water
¹/₂ cup cranberry juice
 cocktail or apple juice
1 tablespoon lemon juice

1 Drain strawberries and raspberries, reserving syrup. In a mixing bowl combine gelatin and boiling water, stirring until gelatin dissolves. Stir in reserved syrup, cranberry juice cocktail, and lemon juice. Chill about 45 minutes or until partially set (the consistency of unbeaten egg whites).

2 Fold in strawberries and raspberries. Pour into a 5- or 5½-cup mold. Cover; chill 4 hours or until firm. Unmold salad onto a serving plate. Makes 8 side-dish servings.

Nutrition Facts per serving: 141 cal., 0 g total fat, 0 mg chol., 32 mg sodium, 36 g carbo., 5 g fiber, 2 g pro.
Daily Values: 46% vit. C, 3% iron

Festive Wreath Salad

4 large fennel bulbs
4 to 8 red sweet peppers
2 heads Bibb or Boston
   lettuce, torn (10 cups)
2 bunches watercress
   (2 cups leaves)
½ cup olive oil
⅓ cup balsamic vinegar
1 teaspoon fennel seed,
   crushed
½ teaspoon salt
¼ teaspoon black pepper

1 Discard outer layers of fennel; slice fennel crosswise into thin strips, discarding core. Halve peppers lengthwise; remove seeds. Slice sweet peppers crosswise into thin half rings.

2 To assemble salad, arrange lettuce and watercress on 12 plates. Arrange fennel and sweet pepper on top.

3 For dressing, in a screw-top jar combine oil, vinegar, fennel seed, salt, and black pepper. Cover and shake well to mix. Drizzle dressing over salad. Makes 12 side-dish servings.

Nutrition Facts per serving: 115 cal., 9 g total fat (1 g sat. fat), 0 mg chol., 119 mg sodium, 8 g carbo., 9 g fiber, 1 g pro.
Daily Values: 57% vit. A, 134% vit. C, 4% calcium, 2% iron

Layered Salad

4 cups torn mixed greens
1 15-ounce can garbanzo
   beans, drained
1 cup cherry tomatoes,
   quartered or halved
1 cup thinly sliced fennel
   bulb or celery
1 large yellow and/or red
   sweet pepper, chopped
   (1 cup)
1 cup diced cooked
   turkey ham (6 ounces)
¼ cup thinly sliced green
   onions
1 cup light mayonnaise
   or salad dressing
2 tablespoons milk
1 tablespoon snipped
   fresh fennel tops
⅛ teaspoon ground black
   pepper
¾ cup shredded reduced-
   fat or smoked cheddar
   cheese (3 ounces)

1 Place mixed greens in the bottom of a 2½-quart clear salad bowl. Layer in the following order: garbanzo beans, tomatoes, sliced fennel or celery, sweet pepper, turkey ham, and green onions.

2 For dressing, stir together mayonnaise or salad dressing, milk, snipped fennel tops, and black pepper. Spread the dressing over the top of the salad, sealing to the edge of the bowl. Cover tightly with plastic wrap. Refrigerate for 4 to 24 hours.

3 Before serving, top salad with shredded cheese; toss gently to mix. Makes 8 to 10 side-dish servings.

Nutrition Facts per serving: 283 cal., 11 g total fat (2 g sat. fat), 30 mg chol., 345 mg sodium, 7 g carbo., 1 g fiber, 8 g pro.
Daily Values: 8% vit. A, 35% vit. C, 8% calcium, 7% iron

Berry Spinach Salad

1 10-ounce package frozen red raspberries in syrup, thawed
1/4 cup sugar
2 teaspoons cornstarch
1/2 cup cranberry-raspberry juice cocktail
1/4 cup red wine vinegar
1/4 teaspoon celery seed
1/4 teaspoon ground cinnamon
1/8 teaspoon ground cloves
1 10-ounce package prewashed fresh spinach
1/2 cup broken walnuts
1/3 cup dried cranberries
1/4 cup shelled sunflower seeds
3 green onions, thinly sliced

1 For dressing, place raspberries in a blender container or food processor bowl. Cover and blend or process until raspberries are smooth. Strain through a sieve to remove the seeds; discard seeds.

2 In a medium saucepan stir together the sugar and cornstarch. Stir in the cranberry-raspberry juice cocktail, vinegar, celery seed, cinnamon, cloves, and strained raspberries. Cook and stir over medium heat until thickened and bubbly. Cook and stir 2 minutes more. Transfer mixture to a nonmetal container; cover and chill until serving time.

3 To serve, in a salad bowl toss together spinach, walnuts, dried cranberries, sunflower seeds, and green onions. Drizzle with half of the dressing, tossing to coat. Cover and chill the remaining dressing in a nonmetal container for up to 1 week to use in other salads. Makes 6 to 8 side-dish servings.

Nutrition Facts per serving: 178 cal., 9 g total fat (1 g sat. fat), 0 mg chol., 82 mg sodium, 23 g carbo., 3 g fiber, 4 g pro.
Daily Values: 33% vit. A, 31% vit. C, 5% calcium, 13% iron

Marinated Peppers and Broccoli

2 pounds broccoli
1/3 cup white vinegar
1/3 cup olive oil or salad oil
2 tablespoons sugar
1/2 teaspoon dried tarragon, crushed
1/2 teaspoon dried thyme, crushed
1/2 teaspoon salt
1/2 teaspoon dry mustard
1 7-ounce jar roasted red sweet peppers, drained and cut into bite-size pieces
Lettuce

1 Wash broccoli; trim off tough ends. Cut broccoli into spears. Cook broccoli, covered, in a small amount of boiling salted water about 8 minutes or until crisp-tender; drain. Cover; chill 4 to 24 hours.

2 For marinade, combine vinegar, oil, sugar, tarragon, thyme, salt, and mustard. Stir in the roasted peppers. Cover; chill 4 to 24 hours. Arrange broccoli on a platter lined with lettuce. Spoon pepper mixture atop. Makes 8 to 10 side-dish servings.

Nutrition Facts per serving: 125 cal., 9 g total fat (1 g sat. fat), 0 mg chol., 158 mg sodium, 10 g carbo., 4 g fiber, 3 g pro.
Daily Values: 28% vit. A, 201% vit. C, 4% calcium, 9% iron

Green Beans with Pepper Butter

Green Beans with Pepper Butter

1 tablespoon butter or margarine

1 medium yellow sweet pepper, coarsely shredded

6 tablespoons butter or margarine, softened

¼ cup pine nuts

1 tablespoon lemon juice

¼ teaspoon salt

⅛ teaspoon black pepper

1½ pounds green beans, trimmed

1 large yellow sweet pepper, cut into thin strips

1 In a small saucepan melt the 1 tablespoon butter or margarine. Add the shredded sweet pepper. Cook over medium-high heat for 5 minutes or until crisp-tender. Set aside.

2 In a blender container or food processor bowl, combine the 6 tablespoons softened butter or margarine and the pine nuts. Cover; blend or process until almost smooth. Add cooked sweet pepper, lemon juice, salt, and black pepper. Cover; blend or process until almost smooth. Set aside.

3 In a covered saucepan cook beans in a small amount of boiling water for 12 minutes. Add the sweet pepper strips the last 3 minutes of cooking. Drain.

4 To serve, transfer beans and sweet pepper strips to a serving bowl. Add the blended butter mixture; toss gently to coat. Makes 8 side-dish servings.

Nutrition Facts per serving: 159 cal., 13 g total fat (7 g sat. fat), 27 mg chol., 71 mg sodium, 11 g carbo., 2 g fiber, 3 g pro.

Daily Values: 160% vit. A, 180% vit. C, 4% calcium, 10% iron

Peas and Onions with Dill Butter

1 16-ounce package frozen small whole onions

2 6-ounce packages frozen pea pods

2 cloves garlic, minced or 1 teaspoon bottled minced garlic

3 tablespoons butter or margarine

1 tablespoon snipped fresh dill or 1 teaspoon dried dillweed

½ teaspoon salt

¼ teaspoon white pepper Fresh dill sprigs (optional)

1 In a large saucepan cook onions in a small amount of boiling water for 2 minutes. Add pea pods and cook 2 to 3 minutes more or just until tender, stirring occasionally. Drain.

2 Meanwhile, in a small saucepan cook garlic in hot butter for 30 seconds. Stir in dill, salt, and white pepper. Drizzle over vegetables, tossing to coat. Garnish with fresh dill sprigs, if desired. Makes 10 to 12 side-dish servings.

Nutrition Facts per serving: 64 cal., 4 g total fat (2 g sat. fat), 9 mg chol., 144 mg sodium, 7 g carbo., 2 g fiber, 2 g pro.

Daily Values: 3% vit. A, 14% vit. C, 2% calcium, 5% iron

Wild Rice-Stuffed Squash

2 14½-ounce cans
   reduced-sodium
   chicken broth
1 teaspoon dried thyme,
   crushed
⅔ cup wild rice, rinsed
½ pound leeks, green
   parts removed, ends
   trimmed, chopped
   (1 cup)
½ cup long grain rice
12 small winter squash,
   each about 3½ to
   4 inches in diameter
½ cup dried cranberries
   or currants
½ cup dried apricots,
   snipped
6 tablespoons butter or
   margarine, melted
¼ teaspoon salt
¼ teaspoon black pepper

1 In a large saucepan bring chicken broth and thyme to boiling. Add uncooked wild rice; reduce heat. Cook, covered, for 30 minutes. Add leeks and uncooked long grain rice. Cover and simmer 15 minutes more or until rice is tender. Let stand, covered, 5 minutes. Drain excess liquid, if necessary.

2 Meanwhile, wash squash. Cut off top third, including the stem, from each. Scrape out seeds with a spoon. Place squash, cut sides down, in a shallow baking pan. Bake in a 350° oven for 30 minutes. Turn cut sides up. Cover pan with foil and bake about 20 minutes more or until tender. Remove from oven; set aside.

3 Stir rice mixture, dried cranberries or currants, and dried apricots together in a large bowl. Stir in melted butter or margarine, salt, and black pepper.

4 Mound stuffing into squash. Place in a shallow baking pan. Bake in a 425° oven about 10 minutes or until heated through. Makes 12 side-dish servings.

Nutrition Facts per serving: 327 cal., 7 g total fat (1 g sat. fat), 0 mg chol., 314 mg sodium, 64 g carbo., 8 g fiber, 10 g pro.
Daily Values: 364% vit. A, 81% vit. C, 16% calcium, 21% iron

Garlic-Mustard Green Beans

2¼ pounds fresh green
   beans (or two 9-ounce
   packages and one
   16-ounce package
   frozen whole or cut
   green beans)
3 slices bacon
1 medium onion, thinly
   sliced (1¼ cups)
3 cloves garlic, minced
4 teaspoons brown
   mustard
¾ teaspoon lemon-pepper
   seasoning or
   ½ teaspoon black
   pepper
¼ teaspoon salt

1 Wash and trim fresh beans, if using. Cook, covered, in very large saucepan with a small amount of boiling water for 20 to 25 minutes or until crisp-tender. (Cook frozen beans according to package directions.) Drain beans; rinse with cold water and set aside.

2 Meanwhile, in a skillet cook bacon until crisp. Remove bacon from pan, reserving drippings in skillet. Drain bacon on paper towels, crumble, and set aside. Cook onion and garlic in drippings over medium heat for 3 minutes or until tender. Stir in mustard, seasoning or black pepper, and salt. Cook about 30 seconds more. Toss beans with onion mixture; heat through. Sprinkle with bacon. Makes 12 side-dish servings.

Nutrition Facts per serving: 42 cal., 1 g total fat (0 g sat. fat), 1 mg chol., 169 mg sodium, 7 g carbo., 3 g fiber, 2 g pro.
Daily Values: 10% vit. A, 19% vit. C, 4% calcium, 5% iron

Peachy Sweet Potatoes

3 medium sweet potatoes
  (1 pound) or one
  18-ounce can sweet
  potatoes, drained
3 tablespoons brown
  sugar
⅛ teaspoon ground ginger
1 8¼-ounce can peach
  slices, drained and
  cut up
1 tablespoon butter or
  margarine
¼ to ½ cup chopped nuts
  or tiny marshmallows
  (optional)

1 Cook fresh sweet potatoes, covered, in enough boiling water to cover, for 25 to 35 minutes or until tender. Drain; cool slightly. Peel potatoes; cut into ½-inch-thick slices. (Or, cut up canned potatoes.) Stir together brown sugar and ginger; set aside.

2 In a 1-quart casserole layer half of the potatoes, half of the peaches, half of the brown sugar mixture, and half of the butter or margarine. Repeat layers. Bake, uncovered, in a 375° oven for 30 to 35 minutes or until potatoes are glazed, spooning liquid over potatoes once or twice. If desired, sprinkle with nuts or marshmallows and bake for 5 minutes more. Makes 4 side-dish servings.

Nutrition Facts per serving: 195 cal., 3 g total fat (1 g sat. fat), 0 mg chol., 45 mg sodium, 30 g carbo., 3 g fiber, 2 g pro.
Daily Values: 196% vit. A, 36% vit. C, 2% calcium, 3% iron

Cauliflower-Broccoli Bake

1 10-ounce package
  frozen cauliflower
1 10-ounce package
  frozen cut broccoli
1 17-ounce can cream-
  style corn
1 10¾-ounce can
  condensed cream of
  celery or cream of
  mushroom soup
1½ cups shredded
  American or process
  Swiss cheese
  (6 ounces)
1 4-ounce can sliced
  mushrooms, drained
1 tablespoon dried
  minced onion
½ teaspoon dried thyme,
  marjoram, or savory,
  crushed
2 tablespoons butter or
  margarine, melted
1 cup soft bread crumbs

1 Cook cauliflower and broccoli according to package directions. Drain; remove from pan.

2 In the same saucepan combine corn, soup, cheese, mushrooms, onion, and herb. Cook and stir until bubbly. Stir in cooked cauliflower and broccoli. Transfer mixture to a 2-quart casserole.

3 Combine margarine and bread crumbs; sprinkle over top of casserole. Bake in a 375° oven for 12 to 15 minutes or until bubbly. Makes 10 to 12 side-dish servings.

Nutrition Facts per serving: 154 cal., 8 g total fat (3 g sat. fat), 13 mg chol., 705 mg sodium, 18 g carbo., 3 g fiber, 6 g pro.
Daily Values: 12% vit. A, 34% vit. C, 11% calcium, 6% iron

Dilly Bread

Dilly Bread

2 cups all-purpose flour
1 package active dry yeast
2 teaspoons dillseed
¼ teaspoon baking soda
2 tablespoons chopped onion
1 tablespoon butter or margarine
1 cup cream-style cottage cheese
¼ cup water
2 tablespoons sugar
½ teaspoon salt
1 egg

1 Generously grease a 1½-quart soufflé dish or casserole or a 9×1½-inch round baking pan. In a large mixing bowl combine ¾ cup of the flour, the yeast, dillseed, and baking soda. Set aside.

2 In a medium saucepan cook onion in the butter or margarine until tender. Add cottage cheese, water, sugar, and salt to onion mixture. Heat and stir just until warm (120° to 130°). Add to dry mixture in mixing bowl; add egg. Beat with an electric mixer on low speed for 30 seconds, scraping side of bowl constantly. Beat on high speed for 3 minutes. Using a wooden spoon, stir in the remaining flour.

3 Spread batter into the prepared pan or casserole. Cover; let rise in warm place until nearly double in size (50 to 60 minutes).

4 Bake in a 375° oven about 25 minutes or until golden brown. If necessary, cover with foil the last 10 minutes of baking to prevent overbrowning. Immediately remove from pan or casserole. Serve warm or allow to cool on wire rack. Makes 8 servings.

Nutrition Facts per serving: 171 cal., 4 g total fat (1 g sat. fat), 31 mg chol., 305 mg sodium, 27 g carbo., 1 g fiber, 8 g pro.

Daily Values: 4% vit. A, 2% calcium, 11% iron

Whole Wheat Brick Alley Bread

1 cup whole wheat flour
1 cup all-purpose flour
1½ teaspoons baking powder
¾ teaspoon salt
½ teaspoon baking soda
1 egg, beaten
1 cup buttermilk or sour milk
3 tablespoons honey
1 cup raisins
1 egg white, beaten

1 In a large mixing bowl combine whole wheat flour, all-purpose flour, baking powder, salt, and baking soda. Make a well in center of dry mixture; set aside.

2 In a small mixing bowl combine the egg, buttermilk, and honey. Add egg mixture all at once to dry mixture. Stir just until moistened. Stir in raisins.

3 Turn dough out onto a greased baking sheet; pat with wet fingers into an 8-inch round (dough will be wet). Brush with egg white.

4 Bake in a 350° oven about 25 minutes or until golden brown and wooden toothpick comes out clean. (If necessary, cover with foil for last 5 minutes of baking to prevent overbrowning.) Serve warm. Makes 1 loaf (16 servings).

Nutrition Facts per serving: 103 cal., 1 g total fat (0 g sat. fat), 14 mg chol., 196 mg sodium, 22 g carbo., 2 g fiber, 3 g pro.

Daily Values: 5% calcium, 6% iron

Note: To make sour milk, place 1 tablespoon lemon juice or vinegar in a glass meauring cup. Add enough milk to make 1 cup total liquid; stir. Let stand for 5 minutes before using.

Gingerbread-Pear Trifle
(recipe, page 65)

Creamy Lime Tartlets
(recipe, page 69)

Banana Walnut Roll
(recipe, page 64)

Divine Desserts

Be sure to save room for one (or two!) mouthwatering desserts. Whether your preference is luscious cake or pie, creamy cheesecake, or festive cookies, turn these pages to discover recipes for irresistible sweets. They're rich with Americans' favorite holiday flavors: pumpkin, eggnog, peppermint, cranberries, citrus, and chocolate.

Banana Walnut Roll

½ cup all-purpose flour
½ teaspoon baking powder
¼ teaspoon baking soda
1 8-ounce package cream cheese, softened
1 3-ounce package cream cheese, softened
½ cup granulated sugar
1 egg
3 tablespoons milk
4 egg yolks
½ teaspoon vanilla
⅓ cup granulated sugar
1 large banana, mashed (about ½ cup)
½ cup finely chopped walnuts or pecans
4 egg whites
½ cup granulated sugar
Sifted powdered sugar
Vanilla Cream Cheese Frosting
Pecan halves (optional)
Orange peel curls (optional)

1 Lightly grease a 15×10×1-inch baking pan. Line bottom with waxed paper; grease paper. Set aside. In a medium mixing bowl stir together flour, baking powder, and baking soda; set aside.

2 For filling, in a small mixing bowl combine cream cheese and ½ cup granulated sugar; beat with an electric mixer on medium speed until smooth. Add whole egg and milk; beat until combined. Spread in the prepared pan; set aside.

3 In a medium mixing bowl beat egg yolks and vanilla on medium speed about 5 minutes or until thick and lemon-colored. Gradually add the ⅓ cup granulated sugar, beating until sugar is dissolved. Stir in banana and nuts.

4 Wash the beaters thoroughly. In a large mixing bowl beat the egg whites on medium speed until soft peaks form (tips curl). Gradually add ½ cup granulated sugar, beating on high speed until stiff peaks form (tips stand straight). Fold yolk mixture into egg whites. Sprinkle the flour mixture evenly over egg mixture; fold in just until blended.

5 Spread the batter evenly over the filling in the pan. Bake in a 375° oven for 15 to 20 minutes or until the top springs back when lightly touched.

6 Loosen cake immediately from sides of pan and turn out onto a towel sprinkled with powdered sugar. Carefully peel off paper. Starting with a short side, roll up cake, using the towel as a guide but not rolling towel into cake. Cool completely on rack.

7 Spread top with Vanilla Cream Cheese Frosting. If desired, garnish with pecan halves and orange peel curls. Makes 10 servings.

Vanilla Cream Cheese Frosting: In a small mixing bowl combine half of a 3-ounce package *cream cheese,* softened, and ½ teaspoon *vanilla;* beat with an electric mixer on medium speed until light and fluffy. Gradually beat in 1 cup sifted *powdered sugar.* Beat in enough *milk* (1 to 2 tablespoons) to make a frosting of spreading consistency. Makes about ½ cup.

Nutrition Facts per serving: 403 cal., 21 g total fat (10 g sat. fat), 150 mg chol., 204 mg sodium, 49 g carbo., 1 g fiber, 8 g pro.
Daily Values: 15% vit. A, 3% vit. C, 7% calcium, 7% iron

Gingerbread-Pear Trifle

1 14- or 14½-ounce package gingerbread mix
⅓ or ½ cup packed brown sugar
2 tablespoons cornstarch
½ teaspoon ground cinnamon
1½ cups cherry-cranberry drink or cranberry juice
1½ cups frozen pitted tart red cherries
  Easy Lemon Cream
1 29-ounce can pear slices, drained

1 Prepare and bake gingerbread mix according to package directions for cake. Cool. (Gingerbread may be made ahead and frozen, tightly covered, for up to 4 months.) Cut into 1-inch cubes.

2 For cherry sauce, in a medium saucepan combine brown sugar (use ½ cup if using cranberry juice), cornstarch, and cinnamon. Stir in cherry-cranberry drink or cranberry juice. Add frozen cherries. Cook and stir until thickened and bubbly. Cook and stir 2 minutes more. Cover and cool without stirring.

3 To assemble, spoon one-third of the Easy Lemon Cream into a 3-quart clear glass bowl. Add one-third of the cherry sauce. Top with half of the gingerbread. Spoon another third of the lemon cream over gingerbread; top with another third of the cherry sauce.

4 Place pears on top of the cherry sauce. Layer with remaining gingerbread, lemon cream, and cherry sauce. Cover and chill for 2 to 24 hours. Makes 10 to 12 servings.

Easy Lemon Cream: Beat 1 cup *whipping cream* and 1 teaspoon *vanilla* just until soft peaks form (tips curl). Fold in 1 cup purchased *lemon pudding*; stir gently until combined. For a creamier texture, stir in 1 tablespoon *lemon juice* or *milk*.

Nutrition Facts per serving: 414 cal., 14 g total fat (7 g sat. fat), 61 mg chol., 324 mg sodium, 69 g carbo., 2 g fiber, 4 g pro.

Daily Values: 14% vit. A, 22% vit. C, 7% calcium, 16% iron

Granny Cake

3 cups all-purpose flour
2 cups sugar
1 teaspoon baking soda
1 teaspoon ground nutmeg
½ teaspoon salt
½ teaspoon ground cloves
¾ cup butter
2 cups mashed ripe bananas
1 8-ounce can crushed pineapple
3 eggs
2 teaspoons vanilla
1 cup chopped pecans

1 Grease and flour a 10-inch fluted tube pan; set aside. In a medium mixing bowl stir together flour, sugar, baking soda, nutmeg, salt, and cloves; set aside.

2 In a large mixing bowl beat butter with an electric mixer on medium speed for 30 seconds. Add bananas, undrained pineapple, eggs, and vanilla. Beat until combined. Add flour mixture. Beat on low speed until combined. Beat on medium speed for 1 minute. Fold in pecans. Spread in prepared pan.

3 Bake in a 325° oven for 70 to 75 minutes or until a wooden toothpick inserted near the center comes out clean. Cool cake in pan on a wire rack for 10 minutes. Remove cake from pan. Cool thoroughly on wire rack. Makes 12 servings.

Nutrition Facts per serving: 481 cal., 19 g total fat (8 g sat. fat), 84 mg chol., 328 mg sodium, 74 g carbo., 2 g fiber, 6 g pro.

Daily Values: 13% vit. A, 12% vit. C, 2% calcium, 13% iron

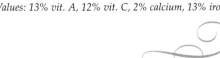

Linzertorte

Linzertorte

2 hard-cooked egg yolks
²⁄₃ cup butter, softened
²⁄₃ cup sugar
1 egg
1 tablespoon kirsch
   (cherry brandy) or
   water
1 teaspoon finely
   shredded lemon peel
¹⁄₂ teaspoon ground
   cinnamon
¹⁄₄ teaspoon ground cloves
1¹⁄₂ cups all-purpose flour
1¹⁄₄ cups ground almonds
   or hazelnuts (filberts)
1 12-ounce jar seedless
   red raspberry jam
1 to 2 tablespoons
   all-purpose flour
   Powdered sugar
   Fresh mint sprigs
   (optional)
   Lemon peel curl
   (optional)

1 Gently press cooked egg yolks through a fine mesh sieve; set aside.

2 In a medium mixing bowl beat butter with an electric mixer on medium to high speed for 30 seconds. Add sugar, egg, hard-cooked yolks, kirsch, lemon peel, cinnamon, and cloves. Beat until thoroughly combined, scraping bowl occasionally. Using a wooden spoon, stir in flour and nuts. Form dough into a ball. Wrap in plastic wrap; chill 1 hour.

3 On a lightly floured surface use your hands to slightly flatten two-thirds of the dough. (Refrigerate remaining dough until ready to use.) Roll dough from the center to edges, forming an 11-inch circle. Wrap dough around the rolling pin. Unroll dough into an ungreased 10×1-inch tart pan with a removable bottom or a 10-inch springform pan. Ease dough into pan, pressing dough about ¾ inch up the sides of the pan. Spread the raspberry jam over the bottom of the dough.

4 On a lightly floured surface gently knead an additional 1 to 2 tablespoons flour into remaining dough until dough is easy to handle. Roll dough into a 10×6-inch rectangle. Using a fluted pastry wheel cut 8 strips each about ¾ inch wide. Lay strips on the filling in a lattice pattern. Trim ends as necessary and gently press ends of strips into rim of bottom crust.

5 Bake in a 325° oven for 35 to 40 minutes or until crust is golden. Cool in the pan on a wire rack. Remove sides of the tart or springform pan. Before serving, sift powdered sugar over top. If desired, garnish with fresh mint sprigs and a lightly sugared lemon peel curl. Makes 10 servings.

Nutrition Facts per serving: 432 cal., 23 g total fat (9 g sat. fat), 99 mg chol., 156 mg sodium, 52 g carbo., 3 g fiber, 7 g pro.

Daily Values: 15% vit. A, 2% vit. C, 7% calcium, 10% iron

Chocolate-Raspberry Torte

12 ounces semisweet
     chocolate, cut up
½ cup whipping cream
¼ cup butter
½ cup sugar
 1 tablespoon all-purpose
     flour
 4 egg yolks
 4 egg whites
½ cup seedless raspberry
     jam
     Sweetened Whipped
     Cream
     Fresh raspberries
     (optional)
     Chocolate Curls
     (optional)

1 Grease an 8-inch springform pan. Line bottom of pan with parchment or waxed paper; grease the paper. Set aside.

2 In a large heavy saucepan combine chocolate, whipping cream, and butter. Cook and stir over low heat until chocolate melts. Remove from heat. Stir in sugar and flour. Using a wooden spoon, beat in egg yolks, one at a time, just until combined. Set aside.

3 In a large mixing bowl beat egg whites with an electric mixer on high speed until stiff peaks form (tips stand straight). Gently fold about 1 cup of the beaten egg whites into the chocolate mixture. Fold chocolate mixture into remaining beaten egg whites. Pour into prepared pan.

4 Bake in a 325° oven for 30 to 35 minutes or until puffed and set about 2 inches around edges. Cool cake in the pan on a wire rack for 30 minutes. Remove sides of pan and cool 4 hours. Chill 4 to 24 hours.

5 Just before serving, remove cake from parchment or waxed paper and place on a serving platter. Heat jam just until melted. Spread top of cake with 2 tablespoons melted jam. Top with Sweetened Whipped Cream. If desired, add raspberries and chocolate curls. To cut torte into wedges, clean knife between slices to prevent dessert from sticking to the knife. Drizzle each wedge with some of the remaining melted jam. Makes 12 servings.

Sweetened Whipped Cream: Chill mixing bowl and beaters of electric mixer in refrigerator. In the chilled bowl combine 1 cup *whipping cream*, 2 tablespoons *powdered sugar*, and ½ teaspoon *vanilla*. Beat with chilled beaters on medium speed until soft peaks form (tips curl). Makes 2 cups.

Chocolate Curls: Carefully draw a vegetable peeler across the broad surface of a *semisweet* or *milk chocolate bar*. This works best if the chocolate is at room temperature. To make ahead, place Chocolate Curls in a single layer on paper towels in a storage container. Cover and store at room temperature or chill.

Nutrition Facts per serving: 381 cal., 26 g total fat (15 g sat. fat), 123 mg chol., 78 mg sodium, 36 g carbo., 2 g fiber, 5 g pro.
Daily Values: 14% vit. A, 2% vit. C, 3% calcium, 10% iron

Creamy Lime Tartlets

Sweet Tart Pastry
1/3 cup sugar
2 teaspoons cornstarch
1/3 cup whipping cream
1 teaspoon finely
   shredded lime peel
2 tablespoons lime juice
1 tablespoon butter or
   margarine
1/4 cup dairy sour cream
Green food coloring
Yellow food coloring
Whipped cream
Finely shredded lime
   peel (optional)

1 For shells, shape Sweet Tart Pastry into eighteen ¾-inch balls. Press balls into ungreased 1¾-inch muffin cups, pressing evenly onto the bottom and up the sides of each cup. Bake in a 400° oven for 8 to 10 minutes or until edges are lightly browned. Cool shells in muffin cups on wire racks for 10 minutes. Remove shells from muffin cups and set aside to cool. (Tart shells may be made ahead and stored, tightly covered, at room temperature overnight or frozen up to 1 month.)

2 Meanwhile, for filling, in a medium saucepan combine sugar and cornstarch. Stir in whipping cream, the 1 teaspoon lime peel, and lime juice. Bring to boiling over medium-high heat, stirring constantly. Reduce heat; simmer for 1 minute, stirring constantly until thickened and smooth. Remove from heat. Stir in butter or margarine, sour cream, and enough food coloring (2 parts green to 1 part yellow) to make the mixture pale green. Cool mixture to room temperature. Spoon into tart shells. Cover and chill for 2 to 4 hours.

3 To serve, spoon a small amount of whipped cream onto each tartlet. If desired, top with shredded lime peel. Makes 18 tartlets.

Sweet Tart Pastry: In a mixing bowl stir together ⅔ cup *all-purpose flour* and 2 tablespoons *sugar*. Cut in ¼ cup *cold butter* until pieces are the size of small peas. In a small bowl stir together 1 beaten *egg yolk* and 1½ teaspoons *water*. Gradually stir egg yolk mixture into flour mixture. Using your fingers, knead the dough until a ball forms. If necessary, cover with plastic wrap and chill for 30 to 60 minutes or until dough is easy to handle.

Nutrition Facts per tartlet: 117 cal., 9 g total fat (5 g sat. fat), 38 mg chol., 41 mg sodium, 9 g carbo., 0 g fiber, 1 g pro.
Daily Values: 7% vit. A, 1% vit. C, 1% calcium, 1% iron

Festive Cranberry-Apricot Pie

Festive Cranberry-Apricot Pie

1 15-ounce package
   (2 crusts) folded
   refrigerated unbaked
   piecrust
½ cup sugar
3 tablespoons cornstarch
1½ teaspoons pumpkin pie
   spice
¼ teaspoon salt
3 15¼-ounce cans
   apricot halves, drained
   and cut into quarters
½ cup dried cranberries,
   snipped
1 egg white
1 tablespoon milk
1 tablespoon sugar
¼ teaspoon pumpkin pie
   spice

1 Using one of the piecrusts, line a 9-inch pie plate according to package directions. Fold edge under. Set aside.

2 In a large bowl combine the ½ cup sugar, the cornstarch, the 1½ teaspoons pumpkin pie spice, and the salt. Stir in apricots and cranberries. Spoon into prepared crust.

3 Place remaining piecrust on a lightly floured surface. Cut with a 2-inch cutter to make 18 to 20 shapes. In a small bowl stir together egg white and milk. Brush egg white mixture over pastry shapes; reserve remaining egg white mixture. Combine the 1 tablespoon sugar and the ¼ teaspoon pumpkin pie spice. Sprinkle half of the pastry shapes with the sugar mixture. Arrange 6 to 8 of the shapes, alternating plain and sprinkled shapes, in a circle in center of the top of pie filling. Brush edge of crust with remaining egg white mixture. Evenly distribute the remaining pastry shapes around edge of crust. Cover edge of pastry lightly with foil.

4 Bake in a 375° oven for 35 minutes. Remove the foil. Bake for 15 minutes more. Cool on wire rack. Makes 8 servings.

Nutrition Facts per serving: 394 cal., 14 g total fat (6 g sat. fat), 10 mg chol., 285 mg sodium, 65 g carbo., 3 g fiber, 2 g pro.

Daily Values: 24% vit. A, 12% vit. C, 2% calcium, 3% iron

Caramel Pecan Pumpkin Pie

Pastry for Single-Crust
   Pie
2 eggs, slightly beaten
1 15-ounce can pumpkin
¼ cup half-and-half or
   milk
¾ cup granulated sugar
1 tablespoon all-purpose
   flour
1 teaspoon finely
   shredded lemon peel
½ teaspoon vanilla
¼ teaspoon salt
¼ teaspoon ground
   cinnamon
¼ teaspoon ground
   nutmeg
⅛ teaspoon ground
   allspice
½ cup packed brown
   sugar
½ cup chopped pecans
2 tablespoons butter,
   softened

1 Prepare and roll out pastry. Line a 9-inch pie plate with pastry. Trim and crimp edge. In a large bowl stir together eggs, pumpkin, and half-and-half or milk. Stir in the granulated sugar, flour, lemon peel, vanilla, salt, cinnamon, nutmeg, and allspice. Pour pumpkin mixture into pastry-lined pie plate. Cover the edge of the pie with foil to prevent overbrowning. Bake in a 375° oven for 25 minutes.

2 Meanwhile, in a medium bowl stir together the brown sugar, pecans, and butter until combined. Remove foil. Sprinkle brown sugar mixture over top of pie. Bake for 20 minutes more or until a knife inserted near the center comes out clean and topping is golden and bubbly. Cool on a wire rack. Cover and refrigerate within 2 hours. Makes 8 servings.

Pastry for Single-Crust Pie: In a mixing bowl stir together 1½ cups *all-purpose flour* and ¼ teaspoon *salt*. Using a pastry blender, cut in ⅓ cup *shortening* until pieces are pea-size. Sprinkle 1 tablespoon *water* over part of the mixture; gently toss with a fork. Push moistened dough to side of bowl. Repeat with 3 to 4 tablespoons additional *water*. Form dough into a ball. On a lightly floured surface, roll dough into a 12-inch circle.

Nutrition Facts per serving: 377 cal., 18 g total fat (5 g sat. fat), 63 mg chol., 188 mg sodium, 50 g carbo., 3 g fiber, 5 g pro.

Daily Values: 123% vit. A, 4% vit. C, 3% calcium, 14% iron

Mint Chocolate Chip Cheesecake

2 cups finely crushed
  chocolate wafers
  (about 36 to 38
  cookies)
1/2 cup butter
2 8-ounce packages
  cream cheese, softened
1 cup sugar
1/3 cup green créme de
  menthe liqueur
3 eggs
3 8-ounce cartons dairy
  sour cream
1 cup miniature
  semisweet chocolate
  pieces
1 ounce semisweet
  chocolate
1 teaspoon shortening

1 In a medium mixing bowl combine crushed wafers and butter; toss gently. Press mixture on bottom and 2 inches up sides of a 9-inch springform pan. Set aside.

2 For filling, in a large mixing bowl beat cream cheese and sugar with an electric mixer on medium speed until combined. Beat in créme de menthe. Add eggs all at once, beating on low speed just until combined. Using a wooden spoon stir in sour cream until combined; stir in the chocolate pieces.

3 Pour filling into crust-lined pan. Set the pan on a shallow baking pan. Bake in a 375° oven for 50 to 55 minutes or until the center appears nearly set when shaken.

4 Remove springform pan from baking pan. Cool cheesecake in pan on a wire rack for 15 minutes. Use a small metal spatula to loosen crust from sides of pan. Cool 30 minutes more. Remove sides of pan. Cool 1 hour; cover and chill at least 4 hours.

5 For topping, melt the 1 ounce semisweet chocolate and the shortening in a small saucepan over low heat. Drizzle chocolate over chilled cheesecake. Chill until set. Makes 14 to 16 servings.

Nutrition Facts per serving: 512 cal., 36 g total fat (21 g sat. fat), 122 mg chol., 296 mg sodium, 39 g carbo., 1 g fiber, 7 g pro.
Daily Values: 24% vit. A, 1% vit. C, 9% calcium, 9% iron

Eggnog Bread Pudding

4 eggs
2 cups canned or dairy
  eggnog
1/3 cup granulated sugar
1/4 cup rum or eggnog
3/4 teaspoon ground
  nutmeg
6 cups dry French bread
  cubes (about 8 slices)
1/2 cup dried cranberries or
  dried cherries
  Sifted powdered sugar

1 In a large mixing bowl use a rotary beater or wire whisk to beat together eggs, eggnog, sugar, rum, and nutmeg. Add bread cubes and dried fruit. Let stand 10 to 15 minutes or until bread is softened, stirring once or twice.

2 Pour softened bread mixture into a greased 2-quart square baking dish. Bake in a 325° oven for 35 to 40 minutes or until a knife inserted near the center comes out clean. Sprinkle with powdered sugar before serving. Serve warm. Makes 6 servings.

Nutrition Facts per serving: 349 cal., 11 g total fat (1 g sat. fat), 142 mg chol., 300 mg sodium, 49 g carbo., 1 g fiber, 9 g pro.
Daily Values: 99% vit. A, 8% calcium, 9% iron

Tiramisu

Hot-Milk Sponge Cake
⅓ cup granulated sugar
2 tablespoons instant espresso powder or instant coffee crystals
⅓ cup water
2 tablespoons rum
2 8-ounce containers mascarpone cheese or two 8-ounce packages cream cheese, softened
½ cup sifted powdered sugar
1 teaspoon vanilla
2 ounces semisweet chocolate, grated
1 cup whipping cream
2 tablespoons coffee liqueur
½ ounce semisweet chocolate, grated

1 Prepare Hot-Milk Sponge Cake as directed. Cool for 10 minutes in pan; remove cake from pan. Cool cake completely.

2 Meanwhile, for syrup, in a small saucepan combine granulated sugar, espresso powder or coffee crystals, and water. Cook over medium heat to boiling. Boil for 1 minute; remove from heat and stir in rum. Cool completely.

3 For filling, in a medium bowl stir together the mascarpone or cream cheese, powdered sugar, and vanilla. Stir in the 2 ounces grated semisweet chocolate.

4 To assemble, cut cake horizontally into 3 layers. Return a cake layer to the baking pan. Brush layer in pan with one-third of the syrup and spread with half of the filling. Repeat layering with the second cake layer, one-third of the syrup, and remaining filling. Top with the third cake layer; brush with remaining syrup.

5 In a chilled bowl combine whipping cream and coffee liqueur. Beat with chilled beaters of an electric mixer on medium speed until soft peaks form (tips curl). Spread whipped cream over top cake layer; sprinkle with the ½ ounce grated chocolate. Refrigerate at least 4 hours before serving. Makes 12 to 16 servings.

Hot-Milk Sponge Cake: Grease and flour a 9×9×2-inch baking pan; set aside. Stir together 1 cup *all-purpose flour* and 1 teaspoon *baking powder*; set aside. In a mixing bowl beat 2 *eggs* with an electric mixer on high speed about 4 minutes or until thick. Gradually add 1 cup *sugar*, beating on medium speed for 4 to 5 minutes or until light and fluffy. Add the flour mixture; beat on low to medium speed just until combined. In a small saucepan heat and stir ½ cup *milk* and 2 tablespoons *butter* or *margarine* until butter melts; add to batter, beating until combined. Pour batter into prepared pan. Bake in a 350° oven for 20 to 25 minutes or until a wooden toothpick comes out clean.

Nutrition Facts per serving: 340 cal., 22 g total fat (13 g sat. fat), 88 mg chol., 75 mg sodium, 31 g carbo., 1 g fiber, 8 g pro.
Daily Values: 7% vit. A, 4% calcium, 4% iron

Pumpkin-Pecan Cheesecake

Pumpkin-Pecan Cheesecake

½ cup finely crushed
   graham crackers
¼ cup finely crushed
   gingersnaps
2 tablespoons finely
   chopped pecans
1 tablespoon all-purpose
   flour
1 tablespoon powdered
   sugar
2 tablespoons butter or
   margarine, melted
2 8-ounce packages
   cream cheese, softened
1 cup granulated sugar
3 eggs
1 15-ounce can pumpkin
1 egg
¼ cup milk
½ teaspoon ground
   cinnamon
¼ teaspoon ground ginger
¼ teaspoon ground
   nutmeg
½ cup whipping cream
   Chopped pecans,
   toasted

1 For crust, in a medium bowl combine crushed graham crackers, crushed gingersnaps, the 2 tablespoons pecans, flour, powdered sugar, and melted butter or margarine. Press evenly onto the bottom of a 9-inch springform pan; set aside.

2 In a large mixing bowl beat cream cheese and granulated sugar with an electric mixer on medium speed until fluffy. Add the 3 eggs all at once, beating on low speed just until combined.

3 Place 1 cup of the cream cheese mixture in a medium bowl. Add pumpkin, the 1 egg, the milk, cinnamon, ginger, and nutmeg. Beat on low speed just until combined. Pour pumpkin mixture into prepared springform pan. Top with cream cheese mixture. With a knife or thin metal spatula, gently swirl through the layers to marble.

4 Place springform pan in a shallow baking pan. Bake in 350° oven for 40 to 45 minutes or until center appears set when shaken. Cool on wire rack for 15 minutes. Loosen crust from sides of pan. Cool 30 minutes more; remove sides of pan. Cool completely. Cover; chill at least 4 hours.

5 Before serving, beat whipping cream until stiff peaks form (tips stand straight). Pipe or spoon into mounds on top of cheesecake. Garnish with toasted chopped pecans. Makes 12 to 16 servings.

Nutrition Facts per serving: 328 cal., 23 g total fat (13 g sat. fat), 132 mg chol., 196 mg sodium, 27 g carbo., 1 g fiber, 6 g pro.
Daily Values: 174% vit. A, 3% vit. C, 7% calcium, 9% iron

Apricot-Hazelnut Biscotti

⅓ cup butter
⅔ cup sugar
2 teaspoons baking
   powder
½ teaspoon ground
   cinnamon
2 eggs
1 teaspoon vanilla
2 cups all-purpose flour
¾ cup chopped hazelnuts
   or almonds, toasted
¾ cup finely snipped
   dried apricots

1 In a large bowl beat butter with an electric mixer on medium speed for 30 seconds. Add sugar, baking powder, and cinnamon; beat until combined. Beat in eggs and vanilla. Beat in as much of the flour as you can. Stir in any remaining flour, the nuts, and apricots. Divide dough in half. If necessary, cover and chill until easy to handle.

2 Shape each portion of dough into a 9-inch log. Place logs 4 inches apart on a greased cookie sheet. Flatten logs slightly until about 2 inches wide. Bake in a 375° oven for 25 to 30 minutes or until a wooden toothpick inserted near the centers comes out clean. Cool logs on the cookie sheet on a wire rack for 1 hour. With a serrated knife, cut each log diagonally into ½-inch-thick slices. Lay slices, cut side down, on an ungreased cookie sheet.

3 Bake in a 325° oven for 8 minutes. Turn slices over; bake for 8 to 10 minutes more or until dry and crisp (do not overbake). Transfer cookies to a wire rack and cool. Makes 32 cookies.

Nutrition Facts per cookie: 96 cal., 5 g total fat (1 g sat. fat), 18 mg chol., 51 mg sodium, 13 g carbo., 1 g fiber, 2 g pro.
Daily Values: 5% vit. A, 1% calcium, 4% iron

Peppermint Pinwheel Cookies

1 cup butter
1 cup sugar
1/2 teaspoon baking
  powder
1 egg
  Few drops peppermint
  extract
2 2/3 cups all-purpose flour
1/4 cup finely crushed
  peppermint candies
  Red food coloring

1 In a large mixing bowl beat butter with an electric mixer on medium to high speed for 30 seconds. Add sugar and baking powder; beat until combined. Beat in egg and peppermint extract until thoroughly combined. Beat in as much of the flour as you can with the mixer. Stir in remaining flour with a wooden spoon.

2 Divide dough in half. To one half of dough add peppermint candies and red food coloring to achieve desired color; mix until thoroughly combined. Leave remaining dough plain. Cover both doughs and chill about 1 hour or until easy to handle.

3 Roll each half of dough between 2 sheets of waxed paper into a 13×11-inch rectangle. Place peppermint candy dough, still between sheets of waxed paper, on a baking sheet. Place in the freezer for 15 to 20 minutes or until firm. (Leave plain dough at room temperature.) Remove from freezer. Remove top sheets of waxed paper from each dough. Carefully invert peppermint candy dough over plain dough, aligning edges. Remove top sheet of waxed paper. Let stand for 5 minutes or until dough is easy to roll.

4 Roll up, starting from one long side, removing bottom sheet of waxed paper as you roll. Pinch to seal. Cut roll in half crosswise. Wrap each half in waxed paper or clear plastic wrap. Chill dough about 4 hours or until firm.

5 Remove one roll of dough at a time from the refrigerator. Unwrap and reshape slightly, if necessary. Cut dough into 1/4-inch-thick slices. Place 2 inches apart on a lightly greased cookie sheet. Bake in a 375° oven for 10 to 12 minutes or until edges are firm. Cool on cookie sheet for 1 minute. Remove and cool completely on wire racks. Makes 50 cookies.

Nutrition Facts per cookie: 77 cal., 4 g total fat (2 g sat. fat), 15 mg chol., 45 mg sodium, 9 g carbo., 0 g fiber, 1 g pro.
Daily Values: 3% vit. A, 1% calcium, 2% iron

Lemon-Nut Madeleines

½ cup sugar
2 egg yolks
½ cup butter, melted and cooled
½ teaspoon finely shredded lemon peel
1 tablespoon lemon juice
½ teaspoon vanilla
½ cup all-purpose flour
½ teaspoon baking powder
⅛ teaspoon baking soda
⅛ teaspoon salt
¼ cup finely chopped toasted almonds
2 egg whites, slightly beaten
Powdered sugar

1 Grease and flour twenty-four 3-inch madeleine molds. Set aside.

2 In a medium mixing bowl beat sugar and yolks with an electric mixer on medium to high speed for 30 seconds. Add butter, lemon peel, lemon juice, and vanilla. Beat on low speed until combined.

3 Sift together flour, baking powder, baking soda, and salt in a bowl. Sift or sprinkle flour mixture over the egg yolk mixture; gently fold in. Fold in almonds. Gently stir in egg whites. Spoon batter into prepared molds, filling each about half full.

4 Bake in a 375° oven for 10 to 12 minutes or until edges are golden and tops spring back when lightly touched. Cool in molds for 1 minute. Using the point of a knife, loosen cookies from molds; invert onto a wire rack. Remove molds and cool cookies completely on rack.

5 Cover tightly and store at room temperature up to 3 days. To serve, sift powdered sugar over tops of cookies. Makes 24 cookies.

Nutrition Facts per cookie: 76 cal., 5 g total fat (3 g sat. fat), 29 mg chol., 74 mg sodium, 6 g carbo., 0 g fiber, 1 g pro.
Daily Values: 4% vit. A, 1% vit. C, 1% calcium, 1% iron

Giant Ginger Cookies

4½ cups all-purpose flour
4 teaspoons ground ginger
2 teaspoons baking soda
1½ teaspoons ground cinnamon
1 teaspoon ground cloves
¼ teaspoon salt
1½ cups shortening
2 cups granulated sugar
2 eggs
½ cup molasses
¾ cup coarse sugar or granulated sugar

1 In a medium bowl stir together flour, ginger, baking soda, cinnamon, cloves, and salt; set aside.

2 In a large mixing bowl beat shortening with an electric mixer on low speed for 30 seconds. Add the 2 cups granulated sugar; beat until combined, scraping sides of bowl occasionally. Beat in eggs and molasses until combined. Beat in as much of the flour mixture as you can with the mixer. Using a wooden spoon, stir in any remaining flour mixture.

3 Shape dough into 2-inch balls using ¼ cup dough (or measure dough using a #20 ice cream scoop). Roll balls in the ¾ cup coarse or granulated sugar. Place about 2½ inches apart on an ungreased cookie sheet.

4 Bake in a 350° oven for 12 to 14 minutes or until cookies are light brown and puffed. (Do not overbake.) Cool on cookie sheet for 2 minutes. Transfer cookies to a wire rack; cool. Makes 25 cookies.

Nutrition Facts per cookie: 293 cal., 13 g total fat (3 g sat. fat), 17 mg chol., 129 mg sodium, 42 g carbo., 1 g fiber, 3 g pro.
Daily Values: 0% vit. A, 1% calcium, 9% iron

Trilevel Brownies

1 cup quick-cooking rolled oats
½ cup all-purpose flour
½ cup packed brown sugar
¼ teaspoon baking soda
½ cup butter, melted
1 egg
¾ cup granulated sugar
⅔ cup all-purpose flour
¼ cup milk
¼ cup butter, melted
1 ounce unsweetened chocolate, melted and cooled
1 teaspoon vanilla
¼ teaspoon baking powder
½ cup chopped walnuts
1 ounce unsweetened chocolate
2 tablespoons butter
1½ cups sifted powdered sugar
½ teaspoon vanilla

1 For the bottom layer, stir together oats, the ½ cup flour, the brown sugar, and baking soda. Stir in the ½ cup melted butter. Pat the mixture into the bottom of an ungreased 11×7×1½-inch baking pan. Bake in a 350° oven for 10 minutes.

2 Meanwhile, for the middle layer, stir together egg, granulated sugar, the ⅔ cup flour, the milk, the ¼ cup melted butter, the 1 ounce melted chocolate, the 1 teaspoon vanilla, and the baking powder until smooth. Fold in chopped walnuts. Spread batter evenly over baked layer in pan. Bake about 25 minutes more or until a wooden toothpick inserted in center comes out clean. Place on a wire rack while preparing top layer.

3 For the top layer, in a medium saucepan heat and stir the 1 ounce chocolate and the 2 tablespoons butter until melted. Stir in the powdered sugar and the ½ teaspoon vanilla. Stir in enough hot water (1 to 2 tablespoons) to make a mixture that is almost pourable. Spread over brownies. Cool in pan on wire rack. Cut into bars. Makes 32 bars.

Nutrition Facts per bar: 141 cal., 7 g total fat (2 g sat. fat), 7 mg chol., 76 mg sodium, 18 g carbo., 1 g fiber, 2 g pro.
Daily Values: 5% vit. A, 1% calcium, 3% iron

Almond Butter Crisps

1 cup butter
1 cup sugar
2 cups all-purpose flour
½ cup blanched almonds, very finely ground
1 tablespoon finely shredded lemon peel
1 egg, beaten
1 teaspoon water
5 ounces green candy coating, melted
5 ounces vanilla-flavored candy coating, melted

1 In a medium mixing bowl beat butter with an electric mixer on medium to high speed for 30 seconds. Add sugar and beat until combined, scraping sides of bowl occasionally. Beat in flour until combined. Stir in almonds and lemon peel. Divide dough into thirds. Cover and chill 1 hour.

2 On a lightly floured surface roll each portion of dough until ⅛ to ¼ inch thick. Cut dough into desired shapes with floured 2½-inch cookie cutters. Place cutouts 1 inch apart on an ungreased cookie sheet. Mix egg and water; brush over tops of cookies.

3 Bake in a 350° oven for 8 to 10 minutes or until golden. Cool on cookie sheet for 2 minutes. Transfer to wire racks and cool completely. (At this point, cookies may be tightly covered and stored at room temperature up to 3 days or frozen up to 1 month.)

4 For frosting, dip half of each cookie into either green or white melted candy coating. Dot with some of the other color candy coating. Drag a toothpick through coatings to make a design. Let cookies stand on wire rack until coating is set. Makes about 60 cookies.

Nutrition Facts per cookie: 90 cal., 5 g total fat (3 g sat. fat), 12 mg chol., 34 mg sodium, 10 g carbo., 0 g fiber, 1 g pro.
Daily Values: 3% vit. A, 1% calcium, 1% iron

Index

Index continued